Japanese Americans and Cultural Continuity

Studies in the History of Education
(Vol. 5)
Garland Reference Library of Social Science
(Vol. 990)

Studies in the History of Education

Edward R. Beauchamp, Series Editor

Japanese Americans and Cultural Continuity
Maintaining Language and Heritage

Toyotomi Morimoto

GARLAND PUBLISHING, INC.
New York & London
1997

Library of Congress Cataloging-in-Publication Data

Morimoto, Toyotomi.
    Japanese Americans and cultural continuity : maintaining lan-
guage and heritage / Toyotomi Morimoto.
            p.   cm. — (Garland reference library of social
science ; vol. 990. Studies in the history of education ; vol. 5)
        Includes bibliographical references and index.
        ISBN 0-8153-1767-0 (alk. paper)
        1. Schools, Japanese—California—History—20th century.
2. Japanese language—Study and teaching—California—History—20th
century.   3. Japanese Americans—Education—California—History—
20th century.   4. Japanese Americans—California—Social conditions.
I. Title.   II. Series: Garland reference library of social science ; vol.
990.   III. Series: Garland reference library of social science. Studies in
the history of education ; vol. 5.
LC3173.C3M67   1997
371.829'96'50794—dc21
                                                        96-40289
                                                        CIP

Printed on acid-free, 250-year-life paper
Manufactured in the United States of America

To Machiko, Daniel Tatsuru, and Amie

Contents

Series Editor's Preface

Garland's Studies in the History of Education series includes not only volumes on the history of American and Western education, but also on the history of the development of education in non-Western societies. A major goal of this series is to provide new interpretations of educational history that are based on the best recent scholarship; each volume will provide an original analysis and interpretation of the topic under consideration. A wide variety of methodological approaches from the traditional to the innovative are used. In addition, this series especially welcomes studies that focus not only on schools but also on education as defined by Harvard historian Bernard Bailyn: "the transmission of culture across generations."

The major criteria for inclusion are (a) a manuscript of the highest quality, and (b) a topic of importance to understanding the field. The editor is open to readers' suggestions and looks forward to a long-term dialogue with them on the future direction of the series.

Edward R. Beauchamp

Foreword

American society is in the midst of an extraordinary demographic transformation, which is being driven by the most extensive migration of immigrants and refugees in the nation's history. Major urban regions—from Los Angeles to Miami, and from Chicago to Houston—as well as many small towns and rural areas, be they Lowell, Massachusetts, or La Crosse, Wisconsin, have been changed dramatically. And what has become so visible in the United States has also become apparent in many of the largest metropolitan areas across the globe from London to Tokyo and from Paris to Sydney. The migration of people from one corner of the world to another in search of economic or educational opportunities, political or religious freedom, or physical safety is occurring on an unprecedented scale.

Toyotomi Morimoto's rich and textured study about Japanese-language schools in the United States, although largely historical in focus, has a great deal of relevancy to contemporary immigrant experiences. In using Joshua Fishman's concepts of language maintenance and language shift, he provides us with a wealth of insights on the seemingly familiar, but hardly routine process by which each of these new groups of immigrants and refugees will seek to come to grips with the issue of retaining the language, values, and traditions of the countries they left in the context of acculturating to and establishing a presence in American society. Will they, as Morimoto demonstrates, be like the pre–World War II Japanese immigrant generation in investing heavily in the building of an extensive ethnic community educational system to "nurture and maintain their linguistic and cultural heritage by teaching the mother tongue"? Will they defend these schools and other community cultural programs even if they become controversial objects of racial animosity or invidious political scorn, as was the case for Japanese-language schools in Hawaii, California, and other states? And will other groups continue to encourage, or even compel, their second and subsequent generations to attend these language schools even after they have come to define the uniqueness of their group identities in American society, or other countries, in terms of shared experiences and values that do not necessarily include fluency in the ancestral language?

Morimoto's provocative work is an important contribution to educational research and to American ethnic and race relations scholarship. Although practically all immigrant groups—the Chinese Americans, German Americans, American Jews, and others—established similar language schools, there has been a paucity of historical and theoretical attention devoted to them. Indeed, there has been far greater emphasis placed on assessing the formal educational experiences of these groups in relation to public schools rather than to nonformal educational activities centered in institutions like language schools that the ethnic communities themselves developed and supported. Morimoto's study should encourage other educational historians and social scientists to rectify this imbalance in our understanding of the multiple educational and social learning concerns and issues that immigrant and refugee populations have had in relation to both formal and nonformal schooling.

At the same time, this study is an important addition to the field of American ethnic and race relations. It shares many features with the new historiography in Asian American Studies, which has sought to unearth a number of previously neglected aspects of a "buried" Asian American past. Pioneered by scholars such as Yuji Ichioka, Him Mark Lai, and others, this innovative approach examines major events and relationships in Asian American history not only from the traditional perspective of how Asian Americans were affected by broader social forces and discriminatory laws and actions, but also how Asian Americans responded to them. The most significant and original works of this new approach have used archival materials written by the immigrants themselves, usually in languages other than English. In Morimoto's case this involved the analysis of historical documents and newspapers written in Japanese by the early immigrants that are part of the Japanese American Research Project Collection at the UCLA Research Library. His analysis of immigrant newspapers like the Rafu Shimpo and Hokubei Mainichi provides a heretofore "buried" insider's perspective on the Japanese language schools.

Morimoto has written a first-rate, pioneering study of one of the most compelling issues on the leadership and community agendas of immigrant and refugee populations in this country, as well as elsewhere. It is a work which should be of keen interest to a variety of audiences from educational researchers to policy analysts, and from ethnic organizational leaders to teachers.

Don Nakanishi
Director, UCLA Asian American Studies Center and Professor,
UCLA Graduate School of Education and Information Studies

Preface

We should erect a sign at each port of entry into the United States:
—Welcome to the United States—
We Cannot Speak Your Language
—Paul Simon, *The Tongue-tied American* (1980)

Today we take it for granted that English is the primary language of the United States. Some of us mistakenly consider it the country's official language. But, as most of us are aware, whether to make English the official language of the United States is still under debate. In the first years of the creation of the nation, the founders actually debated the issue of what language should become its official one. Some suggested that Hebrew should be substituted for English; others promoted Greek. These suggestions were probably because Puritan leaders wanted to be freed from the language of the British rulers.[1]

While the practical benefits of English clearly prevailed, this issue of official language is still alive as immigrants from Spanish-speaking countries and Asian countries enter the United States. Ironically, despite the fact that the United States is a nation of immigrants, very few Americans know much, if anything, about the ethnic community schools that strove to nurture and maintain their linguistic and cultural heritage by teaching the mother tongue. This book is an attempt to record the history of one such group that existed from the turn of the century—Americans of Japanese ancestry. In particular, the book focuses on the efforts of their community in California to maintain their linguistic and cultural heritage from the early twentieth century until immediately before World War II. Although emphasis in placed on the prewar situation in California, the book will also touch on what happened during and following World War II.

Looking at the current situation of Japanese Americans momentarily, we find a rather bleak prospect for language maintenance. David Lopez, whose resource book *Language Maintenance and Language Shift in the United States Today* is applicable to different ethnolinguistic communities, characterizes Japanese Americans as more consistently affluent, older, more likely to use English, and as having a higher number of native-born members than other Asian minority groups in the United States. He concludes that the Japanese in the United States are not a language minority, at least not any longer, and that there is no hope for the English–mother-tongue Sansei (third generation) to use Japanese. Furthermore, he predicts that "however much they might like to 'return' to their culture, they will not do it through their ethnic language."[2]

Returning to the prewar period, one sees quite a different picture. First of all, the most distinctive difference lies in that Issei (first generation) were Japanese nationals, whereas the descendants trying to learn Japanese now are the children of non-native Japanese speakers. Second, the circumstances surrounding the Japanese community are totally different. In the post–World War II period, as we will see throughout the book, learning Japanese was rarely seen as an asset in society in general, except during the war emergency period when military demand made it necessary for some Nisei to be interpreters. In fact, in California, Hawaii, and several other states, the operation of foreign-language schools was severely restricted. Presently, in contrast, learning Japanese is certainly not discouraged, nor are there any restrictive measures against learning Japanese. Third, prewar United States–Japan relations were vastly different from the current bilateral relationship. Although the so-called trade war between the two nations has been frequently at issue in recent years, the increasing significance of economic and political interdependence can hardly be disputed. In the prewar years, on the other hand, although relatively favorable bilateral relations were maintained, the Japanese occasionally strongly resented the state and federal discriminatory legislation against their comrades in the United States.

The reader will find mentioned in the chapters that follow the difficulties experienced by the ancestors of the "model minority."

After an overview in the first chapter of language maintenance in several ethnic groups in the United States, Chapter 2 deals with early Japanese immigrants and the education of the Nisei. A brief description of the early Japanese sojourners is followed by a detailed discussion of the San Francisco Japanese schoolchildren segregation incident in the early part of this century. This incident was the first major discriminatory action involving children of Japanese ancestry in the United States. Chapter 2 also covers Japanese-language schools from the first years through 1912, when the first official meeting of Japanese-language school teachers was held in California.

Chapter 3 probes the struggles that the Japanese immigrants and Japanese-language schools experienced both inside and outside the community. I also touch on the Americanization movement of the 1920s that greatly affected Japanese immigrants. This chapter, further, covers the California Private School Control Law and Japanese immigrants' reaction to the legal actions. (The dual-citizenship problem of the American-born Nisei is touched on in this chapter and others.)

Chapter 4 inquires briefly into the economic, social, and political circumstances promoting the idea that the second-generation Japanese Americans should become a "bridge of understanding." The 1930s were a peak for Japanese-language schools in California, in that the mushrooming of these schools actually caused internal friction within the local Japanese communities. Thus, this chapter also explores problematic aspects of the Japanese-language school, as well as nationalist sentiment related to the Japanese-language schools during the prewar years.

Chapter 5 is somewhat different from the previous chapters in that it deals with Nisei in Japan, not in the United States. The phenomenon of sending Nisei to Japan for study in the mid-1930s is the primary topic of discussion here.

In Chapter 6, I touch upon the language and heritage maintenance efforts of the Japanese abroad who are not covered in the preceding chapters, that is, those in Hawaii and Brazil. While finding some different circumstances in these regions, readers will notice that there were also many similarities among the different regions.

In order to compensate for what is missing in historical data on Japanese-language schools in the prewar period, that is, the actual observation of what was going on inside the schools, in Chapter 7 I discuss the results of a school survey and participant observations that I conducted at certain Japanese-language schools in Los Angeles. Although the ethnographic report presented in this chapter cannot reveal what actually happened in pre–World War II language schools, it will give some hints as to what might have occurred in their classrooms. As another aspect of contemporary language and heritage maintenance efforts among Japanese residing in the United States, I present some statistical data concerning *Nihonjin Gakko* (Japanese schools) and *Hoshu-ko* (Japanese supplementary schools) worldwide and discuss such schools in Los Angeles as an example.

As Ichioka and his colleagues point out, most research on the Japanese American experience has been limited to the World War II internment ordeal and sociological works on immigrants that are based primarily on secondary sources. They suggest that our attention be refocused on the immigrants themselves by utilizing Japanese-language source materials.[3] Thus, approximately half of the sources I used for this book are materials written in Japanese, most of which were found in the Japanese American Research Project (JARP), at the University Research Library, UCLA, and two in influential local Japanese-English newspapers—*Nichi Bei Shimbun* (est. 1899) in San Francisco and *Rafu Shimpo* (est. 1903) in Los Angeles.

Translations from Japanese into English, unless otherwise indicated, are mine.

Acknowledgments

A large portion of this book, being historical in nature, depended upon library research, which I started in 1987 as a student assistant for Che-Hwei Lin, Asian and Asian American bibliographer at the University Research Library, UCLA. I was surprised to find that there was a large collection of materials relating to the Japanese in America in the pre–World War II period. Later, I was asked to help librarians of the Special Collection Department to arrange donated materials from the bereaved families of a Japanese journalist and a haiku poet. As I gradually familiarized myself with the works and materials of Issei (first-generation Japanese) and Nisei (second-generation Japanese Americans), my interest shifted toward educational issues of Nisei in the prewar period, especially those having to do with Japanese-language schools. Although I was first impressed with the amount of material deposited in the Japanese American Research Project, I noticed that something was missing, especially in connection with educational problems with the language and heritage maintenance efforts of Japanese immigrants. The main reason for this was the abrupt uprooting of the community in the wake of the Pearl Harbor attack in December 1941 and the discarding or burning of materials written in Japanese due to fears of their being taken as pro-Japanese activities. Nevertheless, materials, books, newspaper articles, and secondary sources kept in the collection helped me reconstruct the educational circumstances surrounding Nisei to some degree. I would like to express my gratitude to Mr. Lin for giving me an opportunity to have access to this rich source. I should also express gratitude to those who donated valuable materials and to those who devoted time and energy in collecting and arranging them for public use.

Every effort has been made to trace the ownership of copyrighted material and to make full acknowledgment of its use. Regrettably, the material in the appendices has been gathered from sources no longer in print and for which it is virtually impossible to locate an entity from which to request permission for its use. If errors or omissions have occurred, they will be corrected in subsequent editions upon notification in writing to the publisher.

In the course of writing this book, I received the generous assistance of many individuals. Professor John N. Hawkins, Russell N. Campbell, and Don T. Nakanishi were reading committee members for my dissertation, on which this book is based. Their guidance and suggestions during the years of my stay at graduate programs at UCLA made it possible for me to finish the dissertation. I also owe appreciation to Professor Harry H. L. Kitano and Concepción Valadez for their guidance as committee members and to Yuji Ichioka and Yasuo Sakata for their assistance based on their deep knowledge of historical materials on Japanese immigrants. Needless to say, the responsibility for errors and misinterpretations is entirely my own.

The number of individuals who contributed to the completion of this work is large. In addition to those mentioned above, my thanks is especially due to the late Yoshichika Nikaido and Michibumi Hashibe of the Kyodo System; Manabu Minami for his help in obtaining primary sources on Japanese-language education in Brazil; and Richard DeNeut, Hugh Gross, Eugene and Joyce Harding, Rick Smith, Chris Friday, Valerie Matsumoto, Brian Hayashi, and Hiroshi Yoneyama for their friendship, comments, and editorial suggestions. I am indebted to Edward Beauchamp, the chief editor of this educational series, who provided the invaluable opportunity to revise my dissertation and publish it in book form, and to James M. Vardaman, without whose generosity, encouragement, and editorial assistance this book would have not seen the light of day. Some portions of this book were published as articles in *Surugadai Daigaku Ronso* [Surugadai University Studies]. I thank the journal for permission to include the articles in this book.

Lastly, I would like to express my heartfelt appreciation to those involved in making this publication possible, especially to my wife and parents.

Japanese Americans and Cultural Continuity

Chapter One
Cherishing Our Heritage
Language and Heritage Maintenance Efforts in
America

> *Now the whole earth had one language and few words. . . . [And
> men said,] "Come, let us build ourselves a city, and a tower with its
> top in the heavens, and let us make a name for ourselves, lest we be
> scattered abroad upon the face of the whole earth." And the Lord
> came down to see the city and the tower, which the sons of men had
> built. And the Lord said, "Behold, they are one people, and they
> have all one language; and this is only the beginning of what they
> will do. . . . Come, let us go down, and there confuse their lan-
> guage, they may not understand one another's speech."*
> —*Genesis* 11: 1–7

The United States is known as an immigrant country with a continuous influx of different nationalities. And yet, it has been taken
for granted that the country has been bound by a single language
since its inception. This was not the case in colonial days, however.
The Continental Congress printed the Articles of Confederation in
German during the War of Independence. The laws of the Com-
monwealth of Pennsylvania were published not only in English but
also in German from 1805 to 1850. In Louisiana, state laws were
written in French and English from 1804 to 1867.[1] While there is
no doubt as to the importance the English language has played in
the United States, I will in this chapter show that other languages
were a major element of the lives of many immigrants.

Among immigrant families who spoke languages other than
English, the linguistic and cultural gap between the first and the
second-generations widened much faster than either expected. It
eventually became insurmountable. As the gap between the two generations widened, parents began feeling that someone ought to slow

down this process. Parents who were busy working in canning factories in Washington or in the fields in California had no time for teaching their children their own language and cultural heritage. They could hardly ask public schools to fill in the gap. Their English was not good enough to convey their message to the schools even if they had tried.

For many immigrant communities, the easiest and perhaps the most conventional way to solve this problem of children's education was to create their own community mother-tongue schools. Although ethnic community mother-tongue schools are by no means a major part of the American education scene today, in the past private ethnic schools played a much more significant role. Different immigrant groups established their own full-day schools to accommodate the educational needs of their second-generation children. The American public school system became a bona fide part of the educational system of the country only in the early twentieth century.

Thus immigrant groups, like the Japanese whose second generation reached school age in this period, did not have to establish their own private all-day schools; the children attended public schools. Unsure about permanent residency in the United States, Issei (the first-generation Japanese immigrants) created Japanese-language schools to provide supplementary education for their children. As the number of Nisei (the second-generation Japanese Americans, born in the United States) increased, so did the language schools. Despite the often-claimed inefficiency of language instruction in the schools and the pressure of the Americanization movement, Japanese-language schools continued to grow in the 1920s and 1930s.

The increase in the Nisei population is one factor for explaining why Japanese-language schools mushroomed in a short period of time. However, it was not the only cause. In several other ethnic communities, the number of supplementary schools did not expand as rapidly as in the Japanese community. Some possible explanations may be found in what Joshua A. Fishman calls "rewards." There are social rewards (enforcing and recognizing membership in the family, community, society, and people); fiscal rewards (jobs, promotions, raises, and bonuses); political rewards (election, appointment, and public acclaim); and religious rewards. Fishman acknowledges that although schools are, to a large extent, controlled by the social, economic, and political milieu, they are also effective in teaching values to different individual students. He believes that ethnic schools contribute to language maintenance because they offer the symbolic reward of literacy, raise issues of moral imperatives by replacing the role of churches, and become the training institutions where minority ethnic community leaders are raised. Although the aim of this book is not to test Fishman's assumptions, you will find these varieties of symbolic reward crucial in the efforts of the Japanese in America to retain a language and heritage of their own.[2]

Whenever two or more linguistic groups are in contact, the phenomenon of a language shift occurs and the challenge of maintaining a former language sets in. While the former occurs rather naturally in many social contexts, the latter requires somewhat artificial efforts. John Edwards believes that language shift is the rule, not the exception, and that language maintenance is affected more by economic factors than cultural factors. He argues against those who place language at the center of ethnic identity by stating: "Indeed, while we lament the decline of some contemporary minority language we often forget that if we took a long enough perspective we would see that virtually all groups have language shift somewhere in their past. Does this mean that everyone's identity is reduced?"[3] He is convinced that people make choices in order to create "the least possible disruption to [their] existing life style."[4] This pragmatic flexibility, he holds, is the key to group continuity.

Edwards maintains that within a language there should be a distinction between what he calls communicative and symbolic functions, the former being "language in its ordinarily understood sense as a tool of communication," and the latter, "language as an emblem of groupness, as a symbol, a rallying-point."[5] These two aspects of language, he states, can be separated. A linguistic minority group can retain the symbolic aspect of its language while losing the communicative aspect. For him the Irish, whose language is spoken by only a few, continue to demonstrate an attachment to symbolic aspects of their language and thus exemplify language as a symbolic rallying point.

Before discussing the language and culture maintenance efforts among the Japanese community, I will delineate the path that different groups of immigrants in the United States followed in their efforts to maintain their linguistic, cultural, and religious heritage. In discussing these issues, I will limit my focus to the immigrants' private educational institutions.

Public Schooling and Cultural Preservation

There seemed to be a strong conviction among the American people, both old stock and newly arrived, that public schooling was essential to achieving their individual goals. Especially for poor immigrants, the education of their children was seen as essential for moving up the social ladder in a hopefully meritocratic society. In the long run, poor immigrants expected that public schooling could create a society with full equality of opportunity for all.

Public schools were also agencies of cultural transmission. They transmitted mainly white Anglo-Saxon Protestant values to immigrant children. At least, in the eyes of some immigrant parents whose cultural background was different from that of the mainstream Americans, the schools seemed to be teaching the Anglo heritage to their children.

Anglo-Saxon values aside, through public school education, immigrant children in the United States have been taught how important it is to be able to speak English and how loyal they need to be toward the Stars and Stripes. American public schools, though their academic efficacy has been questioned time and again, manifested great efficiency in making children proud of being Americans. Under one flag, one is expected to speak the common language and fight for the common cause. However, for some immigrant parents, this was not what they wanted to see happening. From the early days of its history, the United States was characterized by an uninterrupted flow of immigrants who did not speak English.

Those early immigrants who were seriously thinking of returning to their homeland some day felt that the continuity of cultural and linguistic heritage was too precious to discard in one generation. They tried their best to retain their traditions. In particular, German immigrants, whose continuous influx between 1830 and 1890 amounted to a total of 4.5 million immigrants, were well known for their zeal in trying to maintaining their linguistic heritage. They even established their own public schools to achieve that goal. Though few immigrant parents protested against their children's acquiring

English, many at least hoped that their children would become interested in learning their ancestral language and culture, too.

Let us now turn our attention to the history of the schooling in the United States that was not conducted in the public schools.

Sunday Schools

Although Sunday schools were established primarily for denominational education, they share certain commonalities with ethnic community mother-tongue schools. First appearing in the 1790s, Sunday schools in the United States were designed to provide rudimentary instruction to children of the lower working class. The founders of the schools seemed to be more concerned about literacy training for these children than indoctrinating them. However, by the 1830s, these first American Sunday schools disappeared, and there arose a new type of school taught by volunteers who were mostly evangelical Protestants. In this second phase of development, Sunday schools proliferated remarkably along with the growth of the free public schools. By 1830, as Boyran puts it, "the Sunday school was well on its way to becoming a permanent fixture in American life."[6] In fact, the complementary relationship between these two different types of school continued during the 1830s and 1840s.[7]

One noteworthy phenomenon with regard to Sunday schools in early nineteenth-century America was that the most enthusiastic clients of the schools were found among African American adults and children. In New York, for example, African Americans constituted 25 percent of the pupils in the schools registered in the Sunday-School Union Society by 1817.[8] However, with the spread of public schools during the 1820 and 1830s, which resulted in a decrease in the significance of Sunday schools as providers of basic literacy, African American children found less significance in attending these schools. Furthermore, they were hard hit by racial prejudice, particularly after Nat Turner's revolt in Virginia in 1831. Exactly how many African American–run schools were founded is not known, but they replaced the Sunday schools as providers of literary training. However, such schools were controversial, especially in the South. The white majority could not help worrying about the slave's acquiring literacy, which might lead to other riots. According to a survey done in 1832 by the American Sunday School Union, more than half of its 8,268 affiliated schools were in six states: Massachusetts, Connecticut, Rhode Island, New York, New Jersey, and Pennsylvania. On the other hand, only 499 schools were found in the Deep South slave states. This discrepancy among different regions lasted throughout the antebellum years.[9]

The role that Sunday schools played in literacy training decreased as years passed, but the function of the schools as nuclei for church members in urban areas was significant. In rural areas, too, the Sunday school as an educational institution was a gathering place for children and adults alike. The schools also gave moral lessons to those who attended by teaching "punctuality, obedience, self-discipline, and order, all values consistent with requirements of an industrial age."[10]

Catholic Schools

While Protestants of European origin created Sunday schools to serve their religious as well as educational purposes, European immigrants from Catholic backgrounds created privately funded all-day schools. The early Catholic school was often a bilingual school which taught the immigrant children their own respective mother-tongue as well as English. Proponents of Catholic schools believed that they "afford[ed] a much easier pathway for the foreigner to enter the American life than is the case in the public school."[11] After a generation or two, foreign language as a medium of instruction at most of these schools was replaced by English. Immigrant parents themselves wanted their children to learn English as soon as possible for future social and economic advancement.

The history of private Catholic schools is, however, filled with conflict with public school systems. In California, section No.1664 of the state school law in 1864 required that "all schools must be taught in the English language." And as early as 1861, virtually every school seeking public funds was required to use English as the medium of instruction.[12] In the late nineteenth century, three states in New England enacted laws mandating the use of English in all schools. The requirement of English use in schools spread to other states. In 1890, states that required the use of English in private schools included New York, Ohio, Illinois, Wisconsin, Nebraska, Kansas, North and South Dakota, and Massachusetts.[13] By 1909 the following states required the ability to read and write English before a child was allowed to engage in employment: Arkansas, California, Indiana, Kansas, Maine, Maryland, Massachusetts, Michigan, Minnesota, Montana, New Hampshire, New York, Ohio, Oregon, Pennsylvania, Rhode Island, Texas, and Vermont.[14] The attack against non-English usage came not only from outside but also from inside the Catholic church. Some English-speaking clergy tried to restrict non-English instruction in Catholic schools.[15]

Foreign language instruction in public schools was not, however, totally prohibited in California. In 1865, San Francisco City Superintendent of Public Instruction John Pelton authorized so-called Cosmopolitan Schools in which German and French were taught along with English. Composed of 30 percent German, 20 percent French, and the rest American students in 1867, the multilingual/ multiethnic schools received enthusiastic support from the State Superintendent of Public Instruction in 1867. The 1870 Franco-Prussian War, however, gave supporters second thoughts about the merit of the schools. Consequently, the schools had to convert what had been devoted to foreign language instruction to English. The declining popularity of the Cosmopolitan Schools created a situation where French and German immigrants established their own private, community mother-tongue schools. Deutsche Schulbund and the Alliance Française conducted classes weekday afternoons in public schools. Similar arrangements were made for Italian immigrant children. The Italian Free School Society of San Francisco provided immigrant children with weekday afternoon classes at a public school building in North Beach.[16]

The Jewish All-Day Schools

The growth of Jewish all-day schools in the early and mid-nineteenth century partly stemmed from the immigrants' dissatisfaction with the public schools, as was the case with Catholics. They did not want their children to be educated in schools of Christian influence, and they also worried about the possibility of unqualified teachers in the public schools. However, a shortage of qualified teachers also plagued Jewish schools. Ironically, as the system of management of the public schools improved, the popularity of the Jewish schools dramatically diminished. High tuition also prevented the growth of enrollment in Jewish schools.

The founders of Jewish schools had to face opposition from within. Some Jewish leaders questioned the feasibility of creating such schools on the ground that the schools would further social separatism. From the very beginning some rabbis expressed dissatisfaction with the creation of such schools. Some felt the school "converts the Jew into a self-created alien." Others went so far as to say "that it was a waste to transplant into American soil an institution of the medieval ghetto."[17] In fact, there were some Jewish immigrants who actually took action to assimilate themselves quicker into the host society. Jewish immigrants from Eastern Europe attended New York City's Lower East Side Educational Alliance in order to learn English, not to maintain their mother tongue.

Patterned after the *yeshivot,* schools of learning for Jewish students in Eastern Europe, several Jewish schools were established in the United States in the early twentieth century. In New York City, for instance, there were four Jewish parochial schools with a total enrollment of approximately 1,000. In the all-day schools, which consisted of male students only, Jewish studies were taught from nine A.M. through three P.M., followed by regular subjects, which were offered until seven P.M.

After overcoming operational difficulties during the early period, the Jewish all-day schools showed significant growth from the mid–1910s to the 1930s. By 1939, there were 32 Jewish all-day schools in four states and two schools in Canadian provinces with an enrollment of about 7,000.

The real growth of the Jewish schools came after 1940, however. By 1960, 55,000 pupils attended 265 schools, with an average annual growth of 11 schools and 2,000 pupils.[18] Today the Jewish community has the largest ethnic community school network in the United States. Fishman and Markman report that there were 2,560 Jewish schools in the year 1977–78, of which 17 percent were Sunday schools and 64 percent were weekday afternoon schools. They observed that the graduates of the latter schools were invariably unable to speak modern Hebrew.[19]

Chinese Language Schools

Jewish all-day schools had little in common with Japanese-language schools. Much closer to the Japanese situation were schools in the Chinese community. Chinese pupils in California in the early 1860s could not attend regular public schools with their white majority counterparts. Not only Chinese pupils but also African American and Indian pupils were not allowed to enter public schools because of the California School Law of 1860.[20]

According to Kim Fong Tom, the Chinese public school was created by the School Board of San Francisco in 1859 but closed in 1871. Small privately operated Chinese-language schools were at the same time maintained by Chinese immigrants, usually in their own homes. These small language schools were called *kuan* in Chinese, meaning "a private institute under the supervision of a tutor." With an enrollment of twenty to thirty pupils whose ages ranged from seven to eighteen, these schools held classes on weekdays from five to eight in the evening. Subjects taught included Confucian classics, Chinese language, philosophy, calligraphy, and poetry.

In 1886 the first formal Chinese-language school, the Ching School, was created in San Francisco by the Chinese Imperial Government. Under two teachers, about 60 pupils studied four books— essential readers for any Chinese to pass the prestigious civil service examination in China. Thus the main purpose of the school was to prepare the immigrant pupils for success in China. With this objective in mind, the students studied from three P.M. to nine P.M. on weekdays and from nine A.M. to nine P.M. on Saturdays.

The early Chinese-language schools were operated mostly by district associations. Church groups also operated schools, and in Los Angeles there were seven schools, three of them under the auspices of the Chinese Consolidated Benevolence Association and the rest under the direction of different church groups—Presbyterian, Catholic, Congregational, and Methodist. The number of schools decreased to three in 1943—the Presbyterian Church School, the Catholic Chinese School, and the Congregational Chinese School.

Tom summarized the five functions of the Chinese-language schools: family adjustment, cultural diffusion, social and recreational activities, and vocational preparation. The first-generation parents and second-generation children "live under the same roof, yet they are spiritually far apart."[21] Thus immigrant parents expected the Chinese-language school to help fill the communication and generation gap.

In fact, the language school taught not only the Chinese language but also the history of Chinese civilization in order to cultivate children's knowledge and develop respect toward their ancestral land. The school also provided children with a social gathering place where children of the same ethnic origin were able to come together and play together. Teachers in the school, most of whom were Chinese college students, established good rapport with the pupils. These nontraditional teachers, who were less likely to use corporal punishment, were popular with the children.

Strong ties to the immigrants' home country as well as racial discrimination in America played major roles in the creation of these schools. Since the second-generation Chinese had to depend largely on their own community for employment, Chinese language ability was essential. While those who mastered the Chinese language received favorable treatment in the community, those who could not speak the language felt isolated and were called "brainless."[22] The obvious rewards attached to learning the Chinese language greatly enhanced the significance of the language schools.

Despite the schools' peripheral status in society, they did play a significant role in the Chinese community. The first generation strongly believed in the importance of good communication between the two generations and the continuity of traditional culture. The Chinese-language schools, therefore, yielded benefits not only to individuals but also to the general Chinese community.

As was the case with other ethnic schools, Chinese-language schools were not without problems. It is no surprise to find that the second-generation Chinese did not welcome additional instruction at Chinese-language schools. Many of the older children dropped out. One pupil in Los Angeles, for example, was jubilant when his school was torn down. He had good reason—three hours of Chinese instruction every day after regular school sessions.[23] The younger pupils, nevertheless, found pleasure in playing with children of the same ethnicity. Some even preferred being at school to being at home with a strict father.

While Chinese-language schools had many similarities with Japanese-language schools, the different historical contexts in which the two minority groups were placed provided the two groups with different incentives and benefits. Early Chinese-language schools were taken more seriously by Chinese immigrants than early Japanese-language schools were regarded by Japanese immigrants, at least partially because of the former group's traditionally harsh public examination system. Chinese-language schools did not flourish as Japanese-language schools did, however, due to the 1882 Chinese Exclusion Law (see Chapter 2).

Americanization and Foreign-Language Schools

The history of ethnic schools has been a history of legal battles. In the 1920s when nationalistic sentiment grew in the United States, ethnic schools came under racial attack. With the U.S. participation in World War I, pressure on ethnic schools, particularly German schools, intensified. An increasingly strengthened Americanization movement in this period focused on schools teaching foreign languages, labeling them as un-American institutions. Several states, including Louisiana, Iowa, South Dakota, and Nebraska, in various ways directly or indirectly prohibited the instruction of German and other foreign languages. The Americanization Department of the United States Bureau of Education in 1919 "recommended urgently to all states to prescribe that all schools, private and public, be conducted in the English language and that instruction in the elementary classes of all schools be in English."[24] The office, however, did not oppose church services conducted in non-English languages. Nor did it prohibit instruction in other languages "as long as the right of the child to acquire an elementary knowledge of the English language and to receive his education in it is not violated."[25]

Leading Catholic and Lutheran leaders did not disagree with the recommendations. The regulations prohibiting instruction in foreign languages were not strictly applied to Weekday Afternoon Schools and Weekend Schools. The State Supreme Court in Nebraska, for example, ruled in 1919 that there were no regulations in the state to restrict the teaching of foreign languages in supplementary schools.

Of a number of court cases related to foreign-language instruction in private schools, the Nebraska case was significant. The district court for Hamilton County, Nebraska, on May 25, 1920, charged that Robert T. Meyer unlawfully taught the reading of the German language to ten-year-old Raymond Parpart. A legislative act related to the teaching of foreign languages in the state of Nebraska, which was approved April 9, 1919, included the following:

(1) No person in any private, denominational, parochial, or public school shall teach any subject to any person in any language other than the English language; and (2) foreign languages may be taught only to a pupil who has successfully passed the eighth grade.[26]

The Supreme Court of the state declared that "the direct and intentional teaching of the German language as a distinct subject to a child who had not passed the eighth grade" in Zion Parochial School was against state law, which did not conflict with the Fourteenth Amendment. The United States Supreme Court ruled, however, that mere knowledge of the German language would not be harmful to the student. Meyer's right to teach the language and the right of the student's parents to let him conduct the instruction were within the law. While the U.S. Supreme Court acknowledged that the state could control its citizens to a certain extent, it also reaffirmed that an individual has certain fundamental rights which should not be invaded by the state.

The Supreme Court decision was momentous for Japanese-language schools in California. California State Senator Inman in January 1923 had proposed that for four years, starting from September 1, no person could enter a private foreign-language school unless he had finished the fourth grade of public school. The proposal also stated that beginning in 1930, no foreign-language school would be allowed in California. This proposition passed both the House and the Senate of the State of California and reached the Governor. However, the Supreme Court decision prevented him from signing it.

Regardless of the type of school, certain problems seem to be shared by all, including conflicts generated both within the ethnic communities as well as without. The lack of qualified teachers has been a chronic problem for all ethnic schools, as it has for public schools. Partly because of high public expectations, schools are often criticized regardless of the type of institution. This criticism is in a sense a manifestation of a faith parents hold for these educational institutions. When criticism subsides, it may actually be a sign that parents have lost faith in the educational potential of the school.

The ethnic schools this chapter has discussed—Sunday schools, Catholic, Jewish and Chinese All-Day Schools, and Jewish and Chinese language Weekday Afternoon/Weekend Schools—provided various benefits to their ethnic communities. In most cases, heritage

maintenance seems to be more important than language maintenance. Religiously affiliated schools such as Protestant Sunday
schools, Catholic schools, and Jewish schools offered religious rewards as well as social and, to some degree, economic rewards.

In chapters that follow, I will look at the Japanese community
closely, paying attention to what roles language schools played in
terms of language and heritage maintenance in the community. To
be more precise, I will analyze why Japanese-language schools flourished in the 1920s and 1930s. Attention will also be paid to the
external and internal conflicts and struggles the language schools
experienced.

Chapter Two
Early Settlers
Early Japanese Immigrants and Education of the Nisei

How can we live with our differences without, as always heretofore,
being driven by them to tear each other limb from limb? This is at
bottom a question of power, of the relative power or powerlessness of
groups in relation to one another.
　　　　　—Harold R. Isaacs, *Idols of the Tribe* (1975)

The majority of the Japanese who came to the United States before the turn of the century were either students or young male temporary workers. Thus concern for the education of second-generation children was limited to only a handful of the newcomers. Only after they had their own families did education for the children attract the sojourners' attention.

One major incident in connection with the education of the Nisei was a segregation incident in the San Francisco public schools. Japan's victory over Russia in 1905 caught the public's attention and negatively affected its attitudes toward Japanese immigrants. Exclusionistic sentiment was expressed in newspapers and anti-Japanese meetings were held in San Francisco. Although Japanese children were not the first group ordered to attend segregated public schools, their pride was nevertheless severely hurt.

The Japanese-language school was an essential institution for Issei parents indecisive about their residency in the United States. Language schools gradually shifted their emphasis from preparatory education for possible "returnees" to supplementary education for American-born children who would reside in the United States as American citizens.

The Early Japanese Immigrants
The first group of immigrants from Japan went to Hawaii in 1868 without official approval from the newly established Meiji government of

Japan. Japan was in a chaotic state in 1868, when the Imperial government replaced the 350-year-old Tokugawa Shogunate. Estimates of
the number of those first immigrants vary from 48 to 153.[1] The immigrants were called *Gannen-mono* because of the fact that they left Japan
in the first year (*gannen*) of the Meiji era. Mainly recruited from
the Yokohama area, the first group of immigrants were not ready for
the harsh physical labor required on sugar plantations. This unofficial
immigration in fact resulted in failure. The Meiji government did not
allow any laborers to emigrate to Hawaii again until 1884. The first
officially approved immigrant group consisted of 953 people—689
men, 156 men, and 108 children— and arrived at Honolulu on February 7, 1885, followed by almost 1,000 more immigrants by the end
of the year.[2]

The first immigrants from Japan to the mainland United States
came in 1869, a year after the Meiji Restoration, from Aizu
Wakamatsu as political refugees. Led by a German merchant, they
found a place near Sacramento, called Gold Hill, and intended to
settle there. They named the colony Wakamatsu Colony after their
hometown in Japan. The venture was a total failure due to inappropriate soil and weather for tea trees and silk worms. In the meantime, the first Japanese consulate in San Francisco was established in
1870. The consul reported in 1873, "The population of the Japanese male, female, and minor residents in California are 68, 8, and 4
respectively. The monthly wage for an experienced Japanese house-
keeper working for a white family is fifteen dollars. School boys are
offered meals, clothes and a small amount of pocket money."[3]

After the Meiji Restoration in 1868, young people were encouraged by their predecessors to open new worlds for themselves
by coming to the United States. In particular, Fukuzawa Yukichi
was influential in inspiring youths through his newspaper *Jiji
Shimpo* and several other publications. Many youths, some of whom
were relatively wealthy and well-educated, decided to come to the
United States to carve out a career for themselves. The U.S. Census in 1890 shows there were 2,039 Japanese residents in the United
States, among whom 1,147 lived in California. The major cities
where Japanese immigrants resided in 1890 include: San Francisco,
590; Oakland, 85; Los Angeles, 26; Sacramento, 25; Berkeley, 19;
and San Jose, 11.[4] Thus the early immigrants were heavily concen-

trated in Northern California, particularly San Francisco and its vicinity. *Nihon Teikoku Tokei Nenkan* (the Imperial Statistical Annals of Japan) also contains information on the early Japanese immigrants. Of 602 people who were issued passports for travel to the mainland United States in 1890, 198 were students, 184 laborers, 172 commercial businessmen, 15 craftsmen, and 33 others. The average annual number of passports issued for private students between 1884 and 1897 was around 200.[5]

In 1882 the Chinese Exclusion Act, which prohibited Chinese from emigrating to the United States freely, was passed by Congress. This law created a void in the labor market. The act was the first significant legal restriction that prohibited immigration on the basis of national origin. Late nineteenth-century America was characterized by the antagonistic attitudes of old immigrants toward new immigrants. In 1891, for example, Congress enacted an amendment to the act governing immigration and the importation of aliens under contract to perform labor. The act listed the aliens who were excluded from admission into the United States. Aliens excluded were:

all idiots, insane persons, paupers or persons likely to become a public charge, persons suffering from a loathsome or a dangerous contagious disease, persons who have been convicted of a felony or other infamous crime or misdemeanor involving moral turpitude, polygamists, and also any person whose ticket of passage is paid for with the money of another or who is assisted by others to come, unless it is affirmatively and satisfactorily shown on special inquiry that such person does not belong to one of the foregoing excluded classes, or the class of contract laborers excluded by the act of February twenty-sixth, eighteen hundred and eighty-five.[6]

The influx of immigrants from Southern and Eastern Europe as well as from China made old-stock Americans alert to the increasing number of newcomers.

Within this exclusionist atmosphere the Japanese found themselves working as replacements for Chinese laborers. The Japanese laborers, therefore, were destined to inherit the anti-Oriental sentiment, especially in California. Though insignificant in number, the "hordes" of Japanese immigrants were the second "yellow peril" after Chinese immigrants. Japan's victory over Russia in 1905—the first victory by nonwhite people over white people—accelerated the image of the potential peril caused by the yellow race.

As was characteristic of most immigrants in the United States at that time, Japanese immigrants to the mainland United States before the turn of the century were mostly unmarried male students or laborers. And thus significant educational problems were not yet manifest.

The year 1891 was significant because it marked the first time that over one thousand Japanese entered the United States.[7] The year also marked a shift in destination for the new Japanese immigrants. Until the turn of the century, government-sponsored emigration was aimed at Hawaii. After around 1902, however, many of the Japanese immigrants in Hawaii started moving to the mainland. Before 1900, the population of the Chinese immigrants in California was higher than that of Japanese immigrants, but the 1882 Chinese Exclusion Law had a strong effect after the turn of the century. Census data show that in 1920 the Chinese population in California decreased by nearly ten thousand compared to that of a decade before, while the Japanese population increased by over thirty thousand during the same period. In fact, in 1910 the Japanese population of 41,356 exceeded the Chinese population of 36,248. The population gap between the two minority groups widened. In the next decade, Japanese immigrant population jumped to 71,952, while the Chinese populace plummeted to 28,812.[8]

The San Francisco School Segregation Incident

Anti-Oriental sentiment, which existed in California following the arrival of Chinese laborers in the mid-nineteenth century, was gradually directed toward the newly arriving Japanese immigrants. The Union Labor Party proposed segregating Japanese students in 1901, although this did not occur.[9] In February 1905, an exclusionist movement against Japanese children at a public school in Berkeley took place, although this also did not become a big problem.

After the *Plessy v. Ferguson* case in 1896, the "separate but equal" principle did not seem too strange to the public. The 14th Amendment, which clearly states that "no state shall make or enforce any law which shall abridge the privileges or immunities of any citizen of the United States," was not applied to Homer Plessy, a U.S. citizen living in Louisiana. The U.S. Supreme Court supported the Separate Car Act in Louisiana, which clearly violated the constitutional rights of the black citizens in Louisiana. This ruling marked the end of the Reconstruction era in the South and the beginning of the renewed segregation of African Americans. They had to wait more than a half century to get back rights supposedly guaranteed by the 14th Amendment.

In May 1905 the Board of Education in San Francisco resolved that Japanese students be separated from white students to protect white students from pupils of "the Mongolian race." Proponents of the segregation policy pointed out that the majority of the Japanese children were not children but young men. However, only two of the students were over twenty years old. The Japanese students continued to attend public schools until April 1906, when the great earthquake struck and destroyed the city. In the meantime, the Japanese community established two schools, Nihongo Gakuin and Meiji Shogakko, with enrollments of 91 students in the former and 24 in the latter. Interestingly, the Nihongo Gakuin hired four American teachers.[10] Confronted with numerous scandals of its own, the Board attempted to divert public attention by focusing on race and segregating Asian school children.

In October 1905, the Board of Education ordered principals in public schools to send all Chinese, Japanese, and Korean children to the separate Oriental Public School on Clay Street. While Chinese and Korean parents followed these orders, the majority of Japanese parents refused. Soon the news spread to Tokyo and the problem snowballed into a potential international crisis. The Japanese Ambassador to the United States, Viscount Aoki, visited Secretary of State Elihu Root and complained that the Treaty of 1894 between the two nations should protect the rights of Japanese children residing in the United Sates. President Theodore Roosevelt decided to step in by first sending his personal emissary, Secretary of Commerce and Labor Victor Metcalf, to California. The President then expressed concern about the incident in his annual address to Congress. Although his actions satisfied some members of the Japanese community, he was not able to change the attitude of the Board in San Francisco.

Public opinion was mixed. The incident created heated arguments about the legality of the segregation, at Yale and Harvard law schools, for instance. While the faculty of the former insisted that the Japanese were entitled to protection under international law, faculty from the latter argued that the Japanese should not be granted a greater right or privilege than citizens of this country possess.[11] The judicial debate lingered on with no solution in sight. The president therefore determined to solve the conflict through negotiation with the Japanese government. He proposed to the Japanese government to limit the immigration of Japanese laborers to the United States, while promising to solve the San Francisco controversy. Mayor Schmitz and the Board of Education were invited to Washington to discuss the matter. They came to an agreement that Japanese students could attend their respective public schools. In return, however, Japanese immigration was restricted. The law passed by both Houses of the Congress in February 1907 included the following regulations in regard to the admission of children of immigrants:

No child of alien birth over the age of 9, 10, 11, 12, 13, 14, 15, 16 years shall be enrolled in any of the 1st, 2nd, 3rd, 4th, 5th, 6th, 7th, 8th grades, respectively. Whenever any alien children are found to be unable to enter the grades because of their deficiency in such elements as inability in speaking English, such children should be enrolled in special schools or in special classes exclusively established for them.[12]

The Board of Education in San Francisco on October 13, 1906, resolved that it would repeal Article 19, section 1662, of the school law of California, which stated that "principals are hereby directed to send all Chinese, Japanese and Korean children to the Oriental public school, situated on the south side of Clay Street, between Powell and Mason, on and after Monday, October 15, 1906."[13] However, the Board of Education applied this repeal only to Japanese children. Chinese and Korean students were forced to remain in the segregated school. The Board yielded, but enrolled many students of limited language proficiency in special schools or in special classes in school. Alien Japanese-born students in particular (71 out of 93 students) were required to follow the Board's order.

Again in 1909 segregation revisited this area when the California Assembly passed a Japanese school-exclusion bill by a margin of

46 to 28. In practice, the bill did not affect many Japanese students, at least not to a great extent. Although segregation in schools for Japanese students did not actually take place in San Francisco, it did occur in other Northern California cities in later years. Japanese students in Florin, Walnut Grove, Isleton, and Courtland were placed in segregated schools. Bonds were issued for building segregated schools for children of Japanese and Chinese parentage in Isleton in September 1920, Bates Union (Courtland) in November 1920, and Florin in October 1923. As to why there was not greater protest from Japanese immigrants in these areas compared with San Francisco, Reginald Bell offers the following reasons. First, these towns were closer to Sacramento, where anti-Japanese agitation was strong and was often stirred up by V. S. McClatchy of the *Sacramento Bee.* Secondly, these towns were too small to get the attention of the Japanese government. A lack of influential Japanese who could organize protests was also a factor. Bell speculates that the attention of the Japanese government was focused on the Alien Land Laws, noting that further research into this area is needed.[14]

The attitude of the San Francisco Education Board was not necessarily representative of public opinion. Stanford President David Star Jordan and Superintendent of Los Angeles City Schools Ernest Caroll Moore publicly criticized the San Francisco Board of Education. Moore denounced the Board for its insensitivity and prejudice and stated that he did not believe that the action taken by the San Francisco school authorities was representative of public opinion in California. He also described Japanese students as "quiet and industrious in their school work" and said that "principals and teachers believe them to have a most helpful influence upon the other pupils with whom they associate." When San Francisco Superintendent Roncovieri asked support for his segregation policy at a convention of school superintendents meeting in San Diego, his request was turned down.[15]

In March 1907, the President signed an executive order, the purpose of which was to prevent Japanese residing in Hawaii and Mexico from entering the mainland. This so-called Gentlemen's Agreement went into effect in the summer of 1908, despite strong opposition from Japanese immigrants and American labor contractors. The Japanese government cooperated by agreeing not to issue any more passports to laborers. Thus Japanese immigration was limited to merchants, students, and close relatives of those already residing in the United States. After the surge of immigration in the two years prior to 1908, 14,243 in 1906 and 30,824 in 1907, Japanese immigration dropped to 3,275 in 1909.[16]

Exclusionists later found that the Gentlemen's Agreement was not enough to stop an overall increase in the Japanese population in the United States. Under the agreement, many female immigrants, known as "picture brides," were able to come to the United States to become wives of male immigrants already residing in the country. While there were only 410 married women in 1900 out of a total of 24,326 Japanese immigrants, the number increased to 5,581 in 1910 and 22,193 in 1920.[17] Consequently, the number of American-born second-generation children dramatically increased from 4,502 in 1910 to 29,672 in 1920. However, the Japanese government stopped issuing passports to "picture brides" in 1921. The exclusion law of 1924 further halted the rapid population expansion of Japanese immigrants. The population actually dropped 14,148 during the period 1921 through 1928, due to an increased number of those returning and a decrease in the number of new immigrants.[18]

The Nisei

In his discussion of the educational problems of Nisei in Hawaii, Soen Yamashita stated that the first twenty years was a period when the Nisei problem was viewed only from the Issei perspective. In this period, Nisei children worked with their parents to earn enough money to make a triumphant journey back to their home villages. When the Issei later decided to have the Nisei receive more education, they did so with the hope of escaping from the poverty they were facing. Teachers in Japanese-language schools at that time were mostly sent from Japan. Textbooks used at the schools, including those for moral education, were compiled in Japan.

Yamashita believed that only after the first twenty years was the Nisei situation approached from a Nisei perspective. The Issei gradually considered Nisei to be American citizens rather than subjects of Japan. However, the Issei insisted that Nisei should succeed and thus prove themselves to be good Japanese Americans. The Issei believed or wanted to believe "the success of the Nisei would not belong to the Japanese people, but it would be the honor and glory of the Japanese race."[19] Based on this belief, the aim of education for Nisei changed to emphasize Americanization. Issei educators came to feel the necessity of compiling new textbooks for the Nisei.

Kohei Shimano, a representative educator in the prewar period in Los Angeles, noted that the immigrants' hand-to-mouth daily lives prevented them from providing satisfactory education for their children.[20] It was not uncommon to find these children left outside all day to play by themselves. In Los Angeles, church ministers and other individuals established day-care centers as a precursor for Japanese-language schools to compensate for this consequence of dual-income families.[21]

By the time children reached elementary school level, parents had ambivalent feelings about their children's language abilities. They were proud that their children could speak English like other Americans, a goal seemingly unattainable for the parents themselves, but they worried about their children's loss of Japanese-language skills. Parents often spoke to their children in Japanese, while children answered in English. Some parents sent their children back to Japan to stay with relatives and learn Japanese ways. Those parents who could not afford to do so elected to establish their own Japanese-language schools.

Despite the relatively small number of children at first, the education of children was already considered, at least by intellectuals, to be an urgent issue for Japanese immigrants. The *Shin Sekai,* one of the leading newspapers in the San Francisco Japanese community, editorialized that nothing was more important than matters concerning children's education. It commented that the problem of immigrant children's education was the primary concern of the community.[22]

Japanese-Language Schools, 1903–1912

The first Japanese-language school in California was the Nihongo Gakuin, established by Keizo Sano and his wife in San Francisco in 1903.[23] On April 19 of that year, the San Francisco Buddhist Church of Honpa Honganji Bukkyodan created Meiji Shogakko in San Francisco. Meiji Shogakko was closed, however, in 1907. In Sacramento where many early immigrants resided, the Sacramento Buddhist

Church founded Sakura Gakuen as an affiliated institution in November 1903.[24] This school became one of the largest Japanese-language schools in the prewar period. These early schools and their faculties faced many hardships. Sano Keizo, for instance, worked at a jewelry store in order to operate the school. As was the case with almost any group of ethnic schools we have examined, there was also a heated debate about the raison d'être for Japanese-language schools in the immigrant community. Opposition leaders insisted that the creation of these Japanese-language school would add fresh fuel to the anti-Oriental movement already prevalent in public schools. The early Japanese schools were beset with troubles from both within and without. School buildings and instructional materials were all destroyed in the 1906 San Francisco earthquake.

Of eighteen Japanese-language schools established in California between 1903 and 1912, nine were affiliated with Buddhist churches, while three belonged to Japanese associations.[25] The early Japanese-language schools were established mainly in Northern California, particularly around San Francisco and Sacramento. There was only one school in Southern California in this period.

Among these schools there were no unified policies. Some emphasized Japanese education while others attempted to teach American ideals. Although only the Japanese language was taught at some schools, moral education, history, geography, arithmetic, and arts were included at other schools. Tora Uemura, in his publication on the Japanese in North America in the early 1910s, described Japanese-language schools in the early days:

Wherever the Japanese reside, we can find Japanese elementary schools. There are 16 schools in California with an enrollment of over 470 pupils—250 males and 220 females. However, facilities at these schools leave much to be desired. There is no definite policy among the schools. The pupils are badly influenced by the surroundings, particularly by the children of immigrants from southern Europe. Worse yet, the pupils lose the Japanese characteristics and have become psychologically deformed children who insist only on their own individual ideas.[26]

His remark, though somewhat exaggerated, represents the Issei's irritation with the fast-Americanizing Nisei children. The Issei's resentment toward the Americanizing Nisei is documented elsewhere. Tadashi Fukutake, in his study of the influences of Japanese emigrants on their home village, went so far as to say that Japanese-language schools were a result of the narrow-minded patriotism of the Issei and suggested that the more difficult the adaptation to the host country was, the more the Issei would cherish, embrace, and idealize their homeland. The Issei resented the process of de-ethnization of the Nisei and could not bear the fact that the Japanese language, as a marker of the Japanese mentality, was slipping away.[27]

At a first meeting in April 1912, thirty-four Issei educators congregated to discuss a policy for future Japanese-language schools. Those who gathered at the conference agreed that the primary purpose of Japanese-language schools should be to educate active citizens who would in the future reside in the United States. They decided that Japanese-language schools would teach the Japanese language and the current state of national affairs in Japan as a supplementary education for American-born children. For moral education, they decided that they should reflect the gist of the *Kyoiku Chokugo* (the Imperial Rescript on Education), but at the same time should teach pupils positive aspects of the American experience.[28]

The Imperial Rescript on Education states as follows:

Know Ye, Our subjects:
Our Imperial Ancestors have founded Our Empire on a basis broad and everlasting, and have deeply and firmly implanted virtue; Our subjects ever united in loyalty and filial piety have from generation to generation illustrated the beauty thereof. This is the glory of the fundamental character of Our Empire, and herein also lies the source of our education. Ye, our subjects, be filial to your parents, affectionate to your brothers and sisters; as husbands and wives be harmonious, as friends true; bear yourselves in modesty and moderation; extend your benevolence to all; pursue learning and cultivate arts; and thereby develop intellectual faculties and perfect moral powers. Furthermore, advance public good and promote common interests; always respect the Constitution and observe the laws; should emergency arise, offer yourselves courageously to the State; and thus guard and maintain the prosperity of Our Imperial Throne coeval with heaven and earth. So shall ye not only be our good and faithful subjects but render illustrious the best traditions of your forefathers.

The way here set forth is indeed the teaching bequeathed by Our Imperial Ancestors, to be observed by their descendants and the subjects, infallible for all ages, and true in all places. It is our wish to lay it to heart in all reverence, in common with you, our subjects, that we may attain to the same virtue.

The thirtieth day of the tenth month of the twenty-third year of Meiji.[29]

In 1889 the Imperial Portrait was sent to schools nationwide for reverence. From the next year, with the issuance of the Elementary School Regulations and promulgation of the Imperial Rescript, on to the end of World War II, moral education based on the Imperial Rescript played a central role in Japanese education. The reading of the Imperial Rescript became more like a religious ceremony in schools. As Herbert Passin describes in his interesting volume on Japanese education, *Society and Education in Japan,* "The reader had to carry the sacred scroll reverently, hold it in white-gloved hands, and read it impressively and perfectly. So sacred were these symbols that in case of fire they were to be saved before everything else, even at the risk of life."[30]

We do not know, however, to what extent this indoctrinating principle influenced the general public, at least at the turn of the century. As Passin argues, there was strong opposition and resistance among some intellectuals. Thus, we are not sure to what extent Issei educators were affected by the doctrine and to what degree they tried to indoctrinate Nisei children.[31]

At a second conference in California in 1913, educators decided not to include the Imperial Rescript on Education in their statement of purpose, nor *Shushin* (moral education) as a subject matter in the curriculum. Nonetheless, they wanted to retain moral education as a theme to be included throughout Japanese-language, history, and geography instruction. They emphasized that "the goal to be attained in our education is to bring up children who will live and die in America, and as such, the whole educational system must be founded upon the spirit of the public instruction of America."[32] This emphasis on the assimilation of American spirit had clearly, as Yuji Ichioka points out, been discussed by a group called the *Mokuyobikai,* or Thursday Club, in 1910. "The cardinal principle . . . must be principally the assimilation of American customs and manners, supplemented by education in other essential ideas so that they will not forget the motherland."[33] Aside from the Association of

Japanese Language Schools in California, the Board of Educational Investigation was set up by the Pacific Coast Japanese Association Deliberative Council in 1918 for the purpose of studying, investigating, and directing the education of Nisei.

Most of the available historical data on Japanese-language schools has to do with the ideas expressed only by Issei intellectuals and leaders. Therefore, the consensus of opinion about the educational aims of the Japanese-language schools cannot be taken at face value. Under the pressure of racial prejudice, the school officials may have had no other choice but to express an assimilation-oriented official stance concerning education. It is also difficult to imagine that after the 1912 meeting all schools were moving in the same direction, because the official stance was not necessarily reflected in the policies of individual schools. Nevertheless, it may be safe to say that the general opinion of the Issei educators was that Nisei children should be educated as American citizens but should also maintain the good traits of their heritage.

This dual allegiance is best represented by the expressions *Beishu Nichiju* (primary emphasis on America and secondary on Japan) and *Nisshu Beiju* (primary emphasis on Japan and secondary on America). The early allegiance of Japanese-language schools was most likely Nisshu Beiju, whereas the Japanese Educators Association later stressed Beishu Nichiju. As the expressions themselves imply, neither American nor Japanese elements are necessarily discarded. Rather, the educators wanted to maintain both and sought a happy blending of the best from each culture. This ideal was later manifested in such expressions as *Tozai Yugo* (the fusion of East and West) and *Kakehashi-ron* (the principle of bridging) as the notion of the Era of the Pacific came to the fore in the 1930s.

Tsutae Sato summarized the slowly shifting attitude of the Issei toward American education of their children:

Time passes. Children grow. The original purpose of a glorious homebound journey disappears. Even if one returned to Japan, he would hardly find the Japan he had long cherished. Many returned to America again. . . . Gradually, parents came to seriously think about having Nisei children receive American public schooling as the education for future citizens. Some insisted there was no need to establish Japanese language schools and that the teaching of Japanese could be done at home. Yet Japanese language education at home was close to impossible with only a few exceptions.[34]

Sato pointed out that the Issei in the past tended to idealize the white race at the expense of their own race. This inclination, Sato believed, adversely affected Nisei who disliked their own ancestral land. After living for a certain period in the United States, Issei immigrants found some admirable aspects in the so-called land of opportunity as well as persistent racial prejudice against them as a minority group.

The love–hate relationship between the immigrants and the host country is reflected in the Issei's perception of the education of the Nisei. While setting a high value on public education, Issei still kept the Japanese-language schools as a shelter for their own ethnic language and heritage.

Early Japanese-language schools became established as the population of school-age children increased in Japanese communities of Northern California. Facing financial difficulties and many other challenges, the schools nonetheless managed to maintain themselves. Parents who were busy working and thus had no time to take care of their children's education had a definite motive in creating the schools. Parents expected the schools to provide not only language teaching but also the kind of education which could help their children become acquainted with Japanese culture. This is because many early Japanese immigrants intended to return to Japan after achieving their original purpose of earning substantial savings. Some were able to attain this goal. Many could not. As an increasing number of sojourners became settlers, Japanese-language schools flourished. Perhaps, the most immediate benefit that Issei parents obtained through the schools was that they functioned as day-care centers. There was also a socialization factor for both the parents and children. Beyond church and the public schools, Japanese-language schools were expected to fill a gap that was missing in the community. It became a place where parents could share and exchange information.

In short, the Japanese-language schools were established to serve Issei parents' immediate needs. The Nisei children, on the other hand, were generally too young to consider what rewards they might be enjoying. Spending most of their time in public school classrooms and on playgrounds with other American children, the Nisei children, with a few exceptions in segregated schools, unconsciously acquired American values and customs. Often wondering why they

also had to attend a Japanese language-school, the children innocently followed their parents' instructions. The number of language
schools was limited in this early period, and societal pressure against
the schools was actually minimal compared to what they would experience in the years to come.

Chapter Three
Against the Wind
Struggles of Japanese Immigrants

*It is utterly unthinkable that America or an American state should
be other than white. Kipling did not say "East is East" of the United
States, but if the star No. 31 in Old Glory, California's star, becomes
yellow, West may become East.*
  —Marshall DeMotte, "California—White or Yellow?" in
  Present-day Immigration (1921)

Throughout the period prior to World War II, Japanese in California experienced individual and collective discrimination. The 1913
California Alien Land Law was particularly aimed at Japanese immigrants; they were banned from purchasing agricultural land, and
they could not lease such land more than three years. The law was a
shock to the immigrants, some of whom were leaning toward permanent settlement. The 1924 Immigration Act prohibited any "alien
ineligible to [sic] citizenship" from entering the United States. The
immigration act hurt the pride of Japanese in Japan and that of Japanese in the United States, as the San Francisco school incident did in
1906. This time, however, their humiliation was more intense.

Once the United States entered World War I, a movement called
the "Americanization movement" evolved. The movement promoted
activities designed to help foreign-born individuals achieve naturalization by learning English, American history, and the organization
of U.S. government. Extremists within this movement, however, ini-
tiated hostilities toward ethnic schools. Along with German-language
schools, other ethnic community mother-tongue schools became
targets of anti-foreign sentiment. Foreign-language school control
laws were passed in several states. The alarming growth of Japanese-
language schools in California soon caught the eyes of "patriotic"

Americans, and several laws restricting operations of foreign-language schools were introduced to the state legislature. In 1921, the Private School Control Law was enacted in California for the purpose of restricting the further growth of ethnic community mother-tongue schools, especially Japanese-language schools.

Japanese-language schools had to overcome both internal and external difficulties. This chapter deals with struggles the schools faced, including pressure from the Americanization movement, legislative obstacles, dual-citizenship problems, and difficulties in compiling textbooks.

The Americanization Movement

To characterize the Americanization movement as solely a negative movement may be misleading. The movement did contain positive educational programs that helped immigrants grow accustomed to their new environment. However, the movement was not without damaging effects and was quickly taken over by xenophobia. The critical period of Americanization was World War I and the period immediately thereafter. This movement can be considered "one manifestation of the reaction of the native American elements of the population of the United States to the great impact made upon American life by the coming of the so-called 'new immigration' of the period 1880–1914."[1] The original intention was to Americanize immigrants from eastern and southern Europe. However, cheap wages accepted by new immigrants raised hostility on the part of old immigrants. There was also a fear that the increasing numbers of new foreign elements could disrupt the unity of the country. Intellectuals of old American stock stressed "Teutonic Supremacy." The movement supported a number of legislative acts in an attempt to restrict further immigration from non-Teutonic nations.

While economic incentives encouraged some "older" Americans in outright discrimination against the new elements, others sought better solutions. The YMCA, for example, helped thousands of immigrants learn English and the American way of life. Public schools also started assisting the incoming immigrants by offering English and civics courses. In fact, the Federal Bureau of Naturalization supported the progress of the Americanization campaign incorporated by public schools throughout the nation. The teaching of English was a major part of the Americanization program.

As wartime enthusiasm subsided, however, people grew more skeptical of the Americanization movement. The notion of Anglo-conformity came to be challenged, and the concept of America as a "melting pot"—in which individuals became part of a harmonious blend—came to be seen as an inadequate explanation for the process of socialization. Some doubted whether people of many diverse backgrounds could ever become "typical" Americans. Others argued over the definition of "typical American." Nevertheless, at least in California, the Japanese community faced demands to assimilate, and, as we shall see, Japanese-language schools struggled to survive until the mid–1920s.

Japanese-Language Schools, 1913–1927

The rapid increase of the number of Japanese-language schools alarmed Californians. An early survey in 1913 had shown that in California there were 8,174 Nisei (460 Japan-born and 3,742 U.S.-born males and 326 Japan-born and 3,646 U.S.-born females).[2] When representatives of Japanese associations in the Pacific states gathered in 1918 in Seattle, there was little doubt that education for the coming generation would be a priority topic of discussion. At this meeting, Kiichi Kanzaki of Zaibei Nihonjin-kai (the Japanese Association of America) proposed the establishment of Kyoiku Chosa-kai (the Education Survey Committee) within the Pacific Coast Japanese Association Deliberative Council. Under pressure from the Americanization movement, he urged members of the Council to form a committee for the purpose of adjusting the educational policy of the Japanese-language schools so that they would be accepted by American society.

One survey in Southern California revealed that of 23 schools, 16 schools held classes 5 days a week, 1 school held classes 3 days a week, and another school, 6 days a week. In terms of hours, 11 schools held classes 5 hours a week, 4 schools 10 hours, and 1 school each held class 2, 11, 13, and 19 hours per week.[3] Although this is too small a sample from which to generalize the whole picture of Japanese-language schools in California, the findings nonetheless suggest that a typical school from the late 1920s to the early 1930s operated every weekday afternoon from Monday through Friday, with one hour of instruction each day.

The number of Japanese-language schools in California increased to 31 with 52 teachers in 1914 and 40 with 81 teachers in 1920.[4] As the schools became more visible in society, anti-foreign and anti-Oriental advocates spearheaded the movement against the ethnic schools.

Responding to the pressure to Americanize, Toyoji Abe, a member of the Pacific Coast Japanese Association Deliberative Council, advocated the abolition of all Japanese language schools in the United States. At an extraordinary meeting of the Council in February 1920, he insisted that Japanese-language schools had become the focus not only of anti-Japanese activists but also of pro-Japanese supporters. Abe believed that the very existence of numerous Japanese-language schools would place Nisei in an awkward position, since some politicians were trying to strip citizenship even from the American-born second-generation. One member of the Council suggested that the Japanese-language school would sooner or later die a natural death and proposed that language schools, at least in Southern California, operate cautiously so as to remain congruent with the Americanization movement. Since the schools were observing the basic principles of the Americanization movement, he proposed that the schools continue to operate to the extent that they did not conflict with the ideology of Americanism.

Another member opposed abolishing the schools on the ground that the children needed the education to become of use in bettering the relationship between the United States and Japan in the future. Still others argued that termination of the schools was unrealistic and impracticable given the current circumstances of the Japanese community.[5] The debate continued through the next meeting in San Francisco in June of the same year. Abe defended his position by stating that he did not promote abolition of Japanese-language education all together but rather supported refraining from the Japanese patriotism exhibited in some of the schools. In Oregon, he claimed, Japanese-language schools emphasized their function as preparatory schools for public school education. Such preparation in turn, he felt, would eventually eliminate the need for the language schools. One member pointed out the elimination of the language schools would be extremely difficult, particularly the religiously affiliated language schools, since terminating operations of schools might hurt the ability of Japanese Americans to maintain membership in their own churches.

Still another member argued that the low school achievement of Japanese students in public schools in Florin, California, was because Japanese language instruction was conducted in the morning. Although the town of Florin was an exceptional case, every member of the Council seemed to agree that the Japanese-language education should in no way affect the public school education negatively. Thus, the amended proposal stated: "The content and system of the Japanese-language school should be ameliorated for the sake of the children's future and the spirit of Americanism."[6] No concrete proposals were furthered by the Council.

With regard to Japanese-language schools and Americanization, Kanzaki strongly refuted the charge that language schools promoted emperor worship and taught the fundamentals of Japanese state religion. He argued that the scope of the lessons and the length of the school hours would leave no room for instilling such Japan-oriented education. He emphasized that the schools were teaching Japanese only insofar as it furthered family ties and for the social and economic benefits. He believed that the Japanese language was a valuable asset to the United States, in view of its bilateral relations with Japan.[7]

California Private School Control Law

Nineteen twenty-one was a difficult year for Japanese educators. Assemblyman F. D. Mather of Pasadena set forth a proposal to segregate schools for children of Indian, Chinese, and Mongolian descent. By Mongolian, he implied American children of Japanese descent. Although the bill passed both houses, it never became law. Yet another California bill introduced by Assemblyman J. H. Parker of Auburn, called the Private School Control Law, was passed on June 3, 1921, and enacted on August 2, 1921. The law was quite similar to that enacted in Hawaii in November 1920, which restricted the operation of Japanese-language schools there. Major points of the law included:

(1) Anyone who operates a private foreign language school must obtain a permit from the superintendent of public instruction;

(2) the teachers of the school need to possess knowledge of American history and institutions as well as knowledge of the English language;

(3) instruction must not be conducted in the morning before the school hours of the public schools, and instructional hours should not exceed more than one hour each day nor six hours in a week nor thirty-eight weeks in a year; and

(4) the superintendent of public instruction has full power to approve the course of study and the textbooks and to inspect the school.[8]

Applicants were also required to sign an affidavit as a token of their efforts to Americanize students. Sunday schools were exempted from these regulations.[9]

Despite the fact that substantial restrictions were thus applied to operating language schools, the Japanese community reacted coolly to the control law. The *Rafu Shimpo* reported that the control law was not, in fact, as severe as many Japanese had expected. The examination for language school teachers could be taken in Japanese until June 1923. The *Rafu Shimpo* also editorialized that the control law should be welcomed on the grounds that the intervention of the state would help dispel misunderstandings by the general public. Although the overriding principle of the school had been Beishu Nichiju, the editorial stated, the people of California wanted to be sure that the schools were thoroughly oriented toward Americanization. What the people in California were worried about was the inculcation of Japanese nationalism, which, in fact could rarely be found in most of the language schools. As long as there was nothing against the instruction of the Japanese language, there would be nothing to be afraid of.[10]

In order to prepare teachers for the examination, local Japanese Associations in San Francisco, Fresno, and Los Angeles offered lecture series. The Education Department of the Central Japanese Association of Southern California, for instance, held a lecture series from August 19 through September 9, 1921. Lectures were given in Japanese by members of the Department and covered required subjects. Forty-seven participants received certificates upon the conclusion of the lectures. The next year, American lecturers were invited in order to prepare language school teachers for examinations to be held in English in July 1923. There were 264 total applicants from different ethnic language schools, out of whom 181 Japanese, 77 Chinese, and 6 German language teachers passed the examination.[11] Of the total number of 131 Japanese examinees in San Francisco, 98 passed the examination. Teachers in Fresno reportedly attained similar results.[12]

California State Senator Inman in January 1923 proposed that for four years no person would be allowed to enter a private foreign-language school unless he or she had finished the fourth grade of public school. He further proposed that from 1930 on, no foreign-language school be permitted to operate in California. As stated earlier, the Governor did not sign the legislation because of the Supreme Court decision in the Nebraska case. It should also be pointed out that church groups strongly protested the new measure, because such actions would lead to American schools in foreign countries also being closed. Christian groups also feared negative effects on their efforts to proselytize Asian Americans. A petition signed by Edward L. Parsons, Bishop Coadjutor of California, requested that the Governor review fairly the newly revised "Americanization" textbooks of the Japanese Educational Association.[13]

No less important a court case, *Farrington, Governor, et al. v. T. Tokushige et al.* was decided on February 21, 1927, as follows:

The School Act and the measures adopted there-under go far beyond mere regulation of privately supported schools, where children obtain instruction deemed valuable by their parents and which is not obviously in conflict with public interest. The Japanese parent has the right to direct the education of his own child within reasonable restrictions; the Constitution protects him as well as those who speak another tongue.[14]

The Department of Public Instruction of the State of California informed the Japanese Language Association that the foreign-language control law was void. In contrast with a similar case in Hawaii, the Japanese community in California was not especially excited about this development. Yusen Kawamura, a teacher and writer, commented that Japanese-language schools had suffered enough damage. He observed the following effects of the law: (1) the teachers' orientation changed toward Americanism as they prepared for their examinations; (2) schools could not hire individuals who were unable to understand English, and thus employed only a group who had generally favorable opinions about America; (3) the Association of Japanese Language Schools started the compilation of more Americanized textbooks; (4) the restricted instructional hours curtailed effective language instruction; and (5) some schools now faced more severe financial difficulties. What underlies these observations is the reluctant acceptance of the enforced foreign-language control law. This is contrary to statements by other association members and newspaper editorials which supported the outright adaptation of the Americanization movement. It is not surprising to find there was inconsistency of opinion among educators, intellectuals, and ordinary people. However, after the bitter experiences of the 1913 Alien Land Law and the 1924 Immigration Law, Japanese immigrants for the first time experienced the overturning of an unfavorable law. Therefore, they had significant cause to relax for a moment, if not to expect a somewhat brighter future ahead.

The Dual Citizenship Problem

The Americanization movement did not tolerate individuals who were American citizens but also maintained Japanese citizenship. This problem of dual nationality became an important issue as early as 1908. Because of different means of determining one's citizenship in the United States and Japan, Nisei were considered to hold both American and Japanese nationalities. Nisei became U.S. citizens as their birthright, yet they were also Japanese citizens simply because their fathers were Japanese citizens. The dual-citizenship problem was also discussed at the first meeting of the Taiheiyo Engan Nihonjin Kyogikai (the Pacific Coast Japanese Association Deliberative Council) in 1914 in Portland, Oregon, and continued to be one of the main issues at future meetings. They resolved in 1915 to ask the Japanese Consulate to convey their concern to the Japanese government.[15] The Japanese government amended the law in 1916 at the request of the Japanese Association of America. However, the amendment only applied to those under 17 years of age. Those over 17 had to wait until 1924, when the government further amended the law.

Dual citizenship was interpreted by some Americans as a manifestation of split loyalties. Nisei were accused of being "born of alien parents ineligible to citizenship and who to the end hold their allegiance to a foreign imperial government."[16] Marshall De Motte, Chairman of the State Board of Control, was worried about the consequence of dual nationality, as shown below:

If a father is by birth a citizen of Japan so are his children and his children's children, endlessly. A Japanese born in this country married to a white woman produces a progeny not only half breed as to race but half breed as to loyalty.[17]

For him, Japanese-language schools were institutions that counteracted the effect of American public school education. He believed that the language schools were "taught in the main by Buddhist priests, evidently linking up the Japanese language with their religion which includes the worship of their national ruler."[18] V. S. McClatchy, publisher of the *Sacramento Bee,* also pointed out that the Buddhist priests spoke no English and almost invariably knew nothing about America or American citizenship, and that textbooks used were issued by the Mombusho in Japan. He also charged that according to testimony of teachers in public schools, the Nisei children often studied Japanese lessons during public school hours.[19]

Kawakami claimed that "the average American has an innate prejudice against Buddhism, and the anti-Japanese agitators scheme to discredit all Japanese-language schools by dubbing them 'Buddhist schools.'" He further showed an example of "deliberate misrepresentation by anti-Japanese propagandists, politicians, and newspapers." He quoted the *San Francisco Examiner* (March 21, 1921) in which Assemblyman J. H. Parker of Placer County provided a false list of the Buddhist schools in northern and central California ostensibly checked by the State Superintendent of Public Instruction. Kawakami investigated the false list of eight "Buddhist schools" and demonstrated that only one of these eight schools was a Buddhist school while three others were nonsectarian independent schools, two were Christian kindergartens, and two did not exist at all. Furthermore, he indicated that Senator Phelan naively referred to the Buddhist churches in connection with emperor worship. Quoting Reverend Uchida Koyu, bishop and superintendent of the Buddhist mission of North America, Kawakami denounced Phelan for confusing Buddhism and Shintoism and further denied any connection between Buddhist churches and the Imperialistic policy formulated by the Japanese government.[20]

The Japanese Association of America stated:

[These schools] are primarily for the study of the Japanese language and are not intended to perpetuate the traditions and moral concepts of Japan. Of course, these are criticised by hostile Americans. But says Professor Mills, "They are supplementary schools, and at the worst, there is much less in them to be adversely criticised than in the parochial schools attended by so many children of the South and European immigrants. No real problem is yet evident connected with Japanese children on American soil."[21]

The Association stressed that Japanese-language schools were not inculcating Japanese nationalism.

Compilation of Textbooks

The compilation of textbooks for Japanese-language schools was a pressing issue. Much of the content of the textbooks edited in Japan were inconsistent with what Nisei were experiencing in the United States. For example, in the first volume of the Mombusho (Ministry of Education) textbook series, such topics as *haori* (a Japanese half-coat), *hakama* (a divided skirt for man's formal wear), and *Omiya no Yane* (a roof of a Shinto shrine) were included. In June 1913, when the second annual conference of Japanese Teachers of America was held in San Francisco, the compilation of new textbooks was on the agenda. Since textbooks authorized by the Mombusho were inappropriate, new Japanese-language textbooks needed to be compiled specifically for those children who were born and raised in the United States.[22]

Dialogue continued on the publication of new textbooks year after year. At the fifth meeting of the Pacific Coast Japanese Association Deliberative Council, Shimei Fujioka of Nanka Chuo Nihonjin-kai (Central Japanese Association of Southern California) reiterated the need to create a textbook that would be appropriate for Nisei children. He stressed that Japanese-language education was essential for Nisei, but feared that excessive emphasis on *Chukun Aikoku* (loyalty and patriotism toward the Emperor) manifested in the Mombusho textbook would further encourage the rising sentiment of Americanization. Another member of the Council suggested the context of the textbooks did not have to be purely based on Americanization principles, but that the most important matter for him was to teach children universally shared fundamentals of morality.

He proposed to offer a prize for such a moral textbook, with announcements to Japanese and American educators alike. The proposal was rejected due to its impracticality and expense.[23]

The Conference of the Japanese Association on the Pacific Coast passed a resolution which recommended the establishment of an educational research bureau and the publication of special textbooks. The members who attended agreed that the Japanese language be taught only after public school hours. Also, at an Issei educators' meeting in Southern California in 1915, the following resolutions were passed:

(1) The object of our education of Japanese children shall be to make it supplementary to American public instruction, and the curriculum shall be limited to the teaching of the Japanese language.

(2) Every child who comes to a Japanese school, and who is not attending the public school, should be directed to attend the public schools.

(3) The interpretation of anything in the adopted textbooks which may be contrary to the spirit of Americanism should be carefully corrected.

(4) We should endeavor to publish proper textbooks which correspond to the spirit of true Americanism. This proposition shall be presented to the General Conference of the Japanese Associations of the Pacific Coast.

(5) There shall be selected a Committee on Americanization.[24]

At the eighth annual conference of the Japanese Language School Association in 1919, the inappropriateness of the Mombusho textbooks for Nisei was once again discussed. Furthermore, the question of whether they should teach Japanese language only or foster the spirit of *Yamato Minzoku* (the Japanese race) resulted in bitter arguments. Some suggested that new textbooks should be submitted to the State Board of Education, and once approved by the Board, the Association should make it mandatory for every Japanese-language school teacher to use those textbooks.[25]

The Japanese Language Institutes of Northern California held a meeting in Fresno in October 1920. They resolved at the meeting that the Institutes should be supplementary to the public schools in California. Nisei children should be taught in the same system and spirit prevailing in the public schools in order to achieve good citizenship. The conference also resolved the following:

(1) For kindergarten, both Japanese and American teachers shall be employed in order to effectively prepare the children to enter the public schools.

(2) For the children in public schools, the teaching of the Japanese language shall be from half an hour to one hour. This is to facilitate the communication of ideas between parents and children so that they may enjoy home life.

(3) The Language Institutes shall provide playgrounds for the children to encourage healthy sports and avoid the dangers of bad influences from playing on the street.

(4) A committee is to be appointed to revise the text books which will adequately meet the need of the American-born children.[26]

In regard to the last point concerning the revision of textbooks, the conference decided:

(1) to choose one editorial member each from the Japanese Teachers Association of America, the Japanese Teachers Association of Southern California, and the Japanese Teachers Association of Northern California, who would then compile textbooks up to sixth-grade level within a year;

(2) to establish headquarters for the compilation of textbooks in San Francisco, with editors receiving compensation for their work;

(3) as much as possible to seek input from teachers; and

(4) to contact the State Board of Education for advice.

Actual publication did not take place until 1924.[27]

While Japanese educators in California were talking extensively about textbooks without taking action, those in Washington (Beikoku Seihokubu Renraku Nihonjin-kai Kyoiku Iin-kai) edited five volumes of *Nihongo Tokuhon* [Japanese Readers]. Although an editorial in the *Rafu Shimpo* praised the new Japanese-language textbooks, Japanese school educators in Southern California decided not to adopt them.[28] Instead, they chose to compile new textbooks in collaboration with their counterparts in Northern California. The *Rafu Shimpo* criticized Japanese-language school educators because previous experience showed that collaboration with Japanese in Northern California did not necessarily work well. The editorial even implied that they were unsure if Californian educators could compile better textbooks than those edited in Washington.

In August, representatives of both Southern California and Northern California met in San Francisco and reached a general agreement on the preparation of new textbooks:

(1) The prospective textbooks should follow the California Foreign Language Control Law and aim at accurately teaching the Japanese language to Japanese children living in the United States. Thus, the compilation of textbooks would reflect Americanization.

(2) Topics should not be limited to literary works but include many different spheres of life. Materials should parallel the children's psychological development in America.

(3) *Kanji* (Chinese characters) introduced in the second volume would follow usage in the Mombusho textbooks.

(4) A budget of $5,500 was approved ($3,300 for Northern California and $2,200 for Southern California).[29]

The Foreign Language School Control Law was enacted in 1921 in California. It constrained the teachers and regulated textbooks used in Japanese-language schools. Since new textbooks were still just in the planning stage, the Japanese-language educators translated Mombusho textbooks into English and submitted them to the State Board of Education for approval. In response, the State Board ordered several stories cut from the text. It permitted schools to use these textbooks until new editions could be completed. Some materials eliminated from the textbooks included stories on Jinmu Tenno, Matsuri, Toyotomi Hideyoshi, Kotai Jingu, Tachibana-chusa, Yasukuni-jinja, Waga Kaigun, Shuppei Heishi, historical figures and events which the Board feared encouraged Japanese nationalism.

Finally, in August 1923, the eighteen volumes of *Beikoku Kashu Kyoiku-kyoku Kentei, Nihongo Tokuhon* [The Japanese Reader, Approved by the California State Board of Education] were approved by the State Board of Education and subsequently published in April 1924. These textbooks were supposedly used by all the Japanese-language schools in California from 1924 until 1927, when the California Foreign Language School Control Law was voided by the Supreme Court decision on the Japanese-language school case in Hawaii.

However, Yusen Kawamura pointed out that the textbooks were full of misprints. He further stated that volumes nine and above were too difficult, because of the increasing number of kanji (Chinese characters) they included. He suggested that Mombusho textbooks would better serve children if teachers eliminated portions that might be considered irrelevant.[30]

Kando Ikeda, publisher of *Hokubei Hyoron,* contended that there was no need to compile new textbooks, considering that other ethnic minority groups such as Italians and Chinese used textbooks edited in their own countries. He was especially critical of what he considered to be the accommodating attitude of Japanese educators who volunteered to edit the alternative textbooks. Referring to the matter of picture brides, he explained that subservient attitudes would only lead Japanese immigrants to undermine their very existence. He considered *Nihongo Tokuhon* to be less than satisfactory:

As is usually the case with the Japanese Association which hypocritically pronounces that they are doing things for the sake of others, they chose an unprofessional person as an editor of the critically important textbooks. The end result is disastrous as we expected. Despite the huge amount spent for this project, we find numerous deficiencies throughout the textbook. This imperfect edition naturally brought about copious criticisms from all quarters.[31]

He was in agreement with Kawamura that Mombusho textbooks would better serve Nisei children. He argued that in terms of quality and their relatively inexpensive price, Mombusho textbooks were a better choice. Moreover, he insisted that chapters dealing with Chukun Aikoku (loyalty and patriotism) could be interpreted as loyalty to the United States, rather than Japan.

When the Association of Japanese Language Schools in California conducted a brief survey on the use of textbooks in 1931, they found that twenty-two schools were using Mombusho textbooks while seventeen schools continued to use *Kashu Nihongo Tokuhon*. Eleven others used both textbooks and one school used neither.[32] Although acknowledging *Kashu Nihongo Tokuhon*'s intention of serving American-born Japanese children favorably, the Association called for revisions to correct mistakes and change certain contents. *Kashu Nihongo Tokuhon* was revised several times prior to 1941.

A report by the Japanese consul in Los Angeles to the Minister of Foreign Affairs in 1935 reveals that within the sphere of the consulate's jurisdiction there were 117 schools with 9,277 students and 244 teachers. With regard to textbooks used by these schools, 79 schools, a clear majority, used textbooks compiled by the Mombusho, while only three schools continued to use *Kashu Nihongo Tokuhon* exclusively. Eleven schools used both, and five schools used other textbooks. All junior high schools used textbooks approved and authorized by the Mombusho.[33] Thus, it is clear that increasingly schools replaced *Kashu Nihongo Tokuhon* with Mombusho textbooks.

The textbook issue almost always brought about heated debate at teachers' meetings. When the Central California Japanese Language School Association held a meeting in November 1931, creation of a unified policy on the use of textbooks was discussed. School operators hoped that the same textbook could be used across the board in central California so that pupils would not have difficulty when changing schools. However, teachers in different schools had different opinions about which textbook were more appropriate. After heated debate, they decided to take an opinion poll on the issue. The results showed that while twelve teachers preferred the use of *Kashu Nihongo Tokuhon,* only four insisted on the Mombusho version. Yet, the poll was not a final decision on the use of textbook and no resolution was reached at the meeting.[34]

At a joint conference of the Japanese Language School Associations in Fresno in 1936, eight officials were chosen from the Northern, Central and Southern Japanese Language Associations and fifteen editorial staff members were selected to revise the textbooks. The headquarters of the editorial staff was established in the Southern Japanese Language Association and the editor-in-chief was to receive $2,400 in annual salary. A total of sixteen volumes were expected to be compiled at the pace of one textbook per month.[35]

Officials of the Southern California Japanese Language Association acted to raise funds for the revision of the textbooks by holding a joint *undokai* (athletic meet) of all Japanese-language schools in the Southern California region. The huge undokai was held at the Los Angeles Coliseum with the participation of 10,000 people, resulting in a profit of $7,000, which made compilation of the new textbooks possible.[36]

A prospectus for the new textbooks stated the following:

Nihongo Tokuhon *is the textbook for Japanese children born in the United States, based on the premise that the Japanese-language school is a supplementary institution, but which follows the spirit of American education for the sake of educating good and useful citizens. With this premise, the textbook aims at providing Japanese-American children with necessary linguistic and cultural education for their present and future lives.*[37]

With regard to reasons why the newly revised edition was necessary, the prospectus states that the two textbooks compiled in California and Washington had become outdated, since ten years had passed following their compilation. It further points out that the immigrants' opinions were divided over whether to place primary emphasis on American or Japanese education when the first textbooks were edited. Times had changed and the majority of children attending Japanese-language schools were American-born children, so officials were convinced that new textbooks were necessary.

New plans placed primary emphasis on practical, oral, and communicative aspects of the language. Editorial staff members resolved that teaching methodology should shift from a grammar-translation approach to an oral approach. The guidelines also suggested that Japanese should be taught as a foreign language so that textbooks would meet the demands of the third- and fourth-generation children as well.

Although the lack of dates does not allow us to determine specifically when this prospectus was written, it must have been written after the conference in Fresno in April 1936. The proposal was promising and might have had a positive effect on Japanese language education on American soil. Unfortunately, the effort was too late and could not be carried through due to the outbreak of World War II.

As the 1935 survey reveals, the majority of the language schools used Mombusho textbooks rather than the California edition. Mombusho textbooks themselves were revised several times and one version differs from another even in basic ideological tone and content. It may be important, therefore, to know which version was being used. Karasawa has divided the history of Japanese textbooks between the Meiji period and 1945 into the following eight categories: [38]

(1) Translation-based textbooks (1872–1879: Enlightenment).
(2) Textbooks of Confucian influence (1880–1885: Confucian).
(3) Authorized textbooks (1886–1903: Nationalistic).
(4) State-compiled textbooks I (1904–1909: Capitalistic).
(5) State-compiled textbooks II (1910–1917: Imperialistic).
(6) State-compiled textbooks III (1918–1932: Democratic).
(7) State-compiled textbooks IV (1933–1940: Fascistic).
(8) State-compiled textbooks V (1941–1945: Militaristic).

As Karasawa points out, two major ideological themes can be seen in Japanese textbooks in the prewar period. One is an orientation toward modernization: groups (1) translation, (4) state-compiled I, and (6) state-compiled III periods. The other theme consists of pre-modern and ultra-nationalistic textbooks as in (2) Confucianism, (3) authorized, and (5), (7), (8) state-compiled II, IV, and V, respectively. The pendulum swung three times: in the periods from (1) to (2) in the last decade of the nineteenth century, (4) to (5) in the 1910s, and (6) to (7) in the 1930s.

The Japanese American Research Project Collection includes four kinds of textbooks—those compiled and published: (1) in the United States, (2) by the Mombusho, (3) in Japan, and (4) by the Chuo Nihon Kyoikukai (the Central Japanese Education Association) at Tule Lake Relocation Center, Newell, California. It is noteworthy that the textbooks compiled in the United States were not limited to California's *Kashu Nihongo Tokuhon* and Washington's *Nihongo Tokuhon*. In fact, the collection includes textbooks compiled in Hawaii, such as the Japanese Language Reader for intermediate and advanced levels and *Shushinsho* or a moral education textbook published around 1930. Other textbooks published in California were most likely used as supplementary readings. These are: Yusen Kawamura, ed., *Amerika Nihongo Tokuhon* [The American Japanese Language Reader] (1935); Kisaburo Koda, ed., *Beikoku Kashu Kyoikukyoku Tokyo Sentei Kyokasho: Shoni Dai-ni Tokuhon Dokushu* [New California State Series, School Textbook: The Children's Second Reader] (1906); Tokinobu Mihara and Esther Y. Tani, eds., *Japanese Reader* (1940); and Tenji Nakayama, ed., *Haha no Kotoba* [The Mother's Words] (1924).

Although the collection does not include all versions of Mombusho textbooks used in California, it does provide a clue as to which version they used. Mombusho textbooks in the collection include: *Elementary School Japanese History Textbook* (1915), *Elementary School Science Textbook, 6th Grade* (1919), *Elementary School Geography Textbook* (1919), *Elementary School Japanese Language Reader, Books 7, 10–12* (1929–1935), *Japanese Language Reader: Elementary School, Books 1–5, 7–12* (1932–1938), *Elementary School Shushin Textbook, Book 6* (1933) and *Vols. 3–4* (1936–1940), *Koto Shogakko Japanese Language Reader, Book 4* (1935), and *Japanese Language Reader, Book 1* (1941). Some of the middle school textbooks are: *Japanese Language Reader for the Taisho Era* (1918), *Middle School New Japanese Language Reader, Book 1* (1931), *Middle School Shushin Textbook, Vol. 1* (1931), *New Japanese Language Reader for Girls, Vol. 3* (1932), and *Japanese Language Reader, Books 1–3, 5–7* (1934).

To give an example of the contents of these textbooks, *Jinjo Shogakko Kokugo Tokuhon* [Elementary School Japanese Language Reader], Book 7 (1931) contains a chapter (shown in part below) describing the strengths and weaknesses of the Japanese people.

It is our distinguished national talent and the glorious three thousand years of history that made it possible for Japan to have become one of the five greatest powers of the world. Needless to say, we stand alone in the world when it comes to the fine custom of ours—chuko (loyalty and filial piety)—which wholeheartedly makes for commitment to the Emperor and one's parents. The chuko is our fundamental character, and other good traits derive from it . . .

Raised in a small island, thereby enjoying a peaceful life in the land of paradise, we tend to become too reserved, fail to make strenuous efforts, and lead an indolent life. While the mild climate and beautiful scenery make the people kind and gentle, these factors do not help them to cultivate a magnificent and splendid national character. The national isolation policy in the Tokugawa period for over two hundred years especially discouraged the people from developing the country by going overseas. Instead, they idealized the small insular land and became ignorant about global situations. The seclusion resulted in the creation of a people who do not know how to socialize with other peoples and at the same time are not broadminded enough to accept others. Such shortcomings occasionally invite misunderstandings and even discrimination by other people against those of us who migrated to foreign countries. The weak point of the Japanese is this narrow-mindedness. (from Chapter 27, "Strengths and Weaknesses of Our People")

This particular textbook falls into the modernization period, according to Karasawa's categorization. Yet, as he admits, there were limits in the modernization and democratization expressed in the textbooks of the Taisho period. The chapter quoted above still considers the Japanese people loyal subjects and dutiful sons of the Emperor. Although the chapter encourages Japan's overseas expansion, it blames its immigrants for their lack of sensitivity toward host societies. There is no way of knowing how the teacher of the Japanese-language school taught this portion of the chapter to the students. Nor is it possible for us to speculate how the students felt about it. Nevertheless, the chapter seems to reflect a general attitude of the Japanese nationals toward their fellow countrymen living abroad.

Tsukuru Fujimura, ed., *Teikoku Shin Kokubun* [New Japanese Language Reader for Japan], Book 8 (1932) contains a first chapter discussing the Japanese spirit and the world spirit. In it, the author reproves youth for placing themselves first before the life of the nation. He asserts that the basic unit of life is to live as a member of the nation, not as an individual human being. The chapter, however, does stress that one should also aim to become an internationally minded individual. The author emphasizes that extreme positions should be avoided and that a balanced stance accepting East and West ought to be pursued.

Returning to the editorial guideline for the textbooks in California, it placed primary emphasis on practical, oral, and communicative aspects of language teaching. The guideline suggested that Japanese should be taught as a foreign language with American-born Nisei students in mind, so that prospective textbooks would meet demands of the third- and fourth-generation children in the future.

The Arguments for and Against the Japanese-Language School

Reflecting upon the years when anti-Japanese sentiment was prevalent in California, a well-known haiku poet in Los Angeles, Shisei Tsuneishi (1888–1987) referred to the attitude of immigrant intellectuals toward the Japanese-language school:

When the "hai-nichi" or anti-Japanese movement prevailed, relatively well-educated Issei believed that the Japanese language would disappear in the next generation or so. Therefore many of the so-called intellectuals did not send their children to Japanese-language schools, saying that all the expenditures for the school would go down the drain. Not only the school but also the Japanese vernacular newspapers and Japanese signs at the stores would be all gone, they predicted. They were confident that the anti-Japanese sentiment would vanish if and only if all Japanese elements were cast into the American melting pot. We, haiku poets, felt forlorn about the future of haiku under such circumstances.[39]

Those who were reluctant to support Japanese-language schools argued that Nisei students were already burdened with assignments in public schools and that the additional study of Japanese language would create an intellectual overload, detrimental to their work in the public schools. It was also argued that if the students were forced to study Japanese, it would be very unlikely that they would succeed in appreciating the language and culture.

Proponents of Japanese-language schools often stressed the importance of family unity through language communication. A common language, they felt, should be used or at least understood by both generations in order to establish good communication. In the wake of a rise in juvenile delinquency among Nisei youths, community leaders urged parents to make an attempt to provide children with their ancestral language for better communication and, subsequently, to create better citizens of America.[40]

Knowledge of the Japanese language was in many cases a necessity in securing vocational opportunities, for despite their attainment of higher education, few occupational opportunities were available to Nisei. Not only Japanese immigrant parents but also whites suggested that Nisei learn the Japanese language and train themselves for particular occupations.[41]

Ujiro Oyama synthesized the supporting opinions for the Japanese-language school as follows:

(1) It is a natural tendency on the part of the immigrant parents to desire that their children be acquainted with the ancestral language. This is a natural instinct of human beings. The language is necessary for better family life.

(2) Today, everyone in the world needs to be able to speak more than one language. In fact, in the United States, French Americans learn French, Italian Americans learn Italian and German Americans learn German. Others learn different languages for different purposes. Japanese Americans must learn Japanese, for they have few choices but to find jobs which require Japanese language ability. Those who cannot speak Japanese are indeed suffering because of the scarce employment opportunities.

(3) It is essential to maintain sympathetic understanding toward each other's situation, in order to establish a good United States–Japan relationship. The best candidates for mediating such an important relationship are the U.S.-born Japanese children. Thus, providing the children with Japanese-language education is beneficial for both Japan and the United States.

(4) The United States is a country where people from all over the world assemble and create one whole unit. Therefore, it is the responsibility of the Japanese Americans to make the effort of studying Japanese, understanding Japan's culture, and further transplanting its cultural heritage onto American soil. The Japanese American children's attendance at Japanese-language schools should be welcomed by the United States and Japan.[42]

In short, favorable opinions of Japanese-language schools can be divided into two categories: One is an ideological stance, lifting up the position of the Nisei as the "bridge of understanding" between the United States and Japan. The other is based on pragmatic needs, such as better communication at home and better employment opportunities. Whether rewards were ideological or pragmatic, Japanese-language schools were indispensable for the immigrant's daily life.

Before "emancipation" from legal restrictions—in fact, in the midst of nationalistic sentiment in the 1920s—Japanese-language schools developed at an accelerating pace. The number of schools increased, not because more and more immigrants wanted to return to Japan with their U.S.-born children, but on the contrary, because many of the immigrants decided to stay.

The post–1927 period, especially the early 1930s, witnessed the increasing influence of the militant Japanese government over the life of Japanese immigrants in the United States. To what extent the fatherland affected the lives of the immigrants, what differences existed in the responses of first- and second-generations to such influences, and what role Japanese-language schools played in these issues will be explored in the following two chapters.

Chapter Four
Portent of War
Nationalistic Sentiment and Japanese-Language Schools, 1927–1941

Admiral Togo has the Japanese Spirit, so has the man in the street: fish-shop managers, swindlers, murderers, none would be complete, none would be the men they are, none would be a man if he wasn't wrapped up like a tuppenny cup in the Spirit of Japan. . . . Is the Spirit of Japan triangular? Is it, do you think, a square? Why no indeed! As the words themselves explicitly declare, it's an airy, fairy, spiritual thing and things that close to God can't be defined in a formula or measured with a measuring-rod.

> —Soseki Natsume, *Wagahai wa Neko de aru* [I am a Cat]. Translated by Aiko Ito and Graeme Wilson.

From the early 1930s to the outbreak of World War II, the Nisei in America as well as the Issei could not help feeling the mounting tensions in their ancestral land. Local vernacular Japanese newspapers day after day uncritically reported Japanese militaristic aggression in China. Issei leaders along with some Japanese opinion leaders occasionally advocated the amalgamation of the Eastern spiritual civilization and the Western material civilization. They were impressed with American technology while maintaining their pride in the Japanese moral tradition called *Yamato-damashii,* the Japanese spirit. The Issei, considered an unassimilable group of immigrants, called for second-generation Nisei youths to be the "bridge of understanding." Unable to express themselves freely in English, the Issei expected the American-born Nisei to defend the Japanese position and persuade the American public on behalf of the Japanese government. While American society at large was struggling with the aftermath of the 1929 Depression, the Japanese army found itself bogged down in China and increasingly criticized by the West. The Japanese immigrant community naturally could not escape from either of these traumatic events. The Nisei had a difficult time finding jobs and felt pressure from being bicultural as well as bilingual. It was a hard time for most people to find a good job, but it was particularly hard for youths of Japanese ancestry.

Given the gloomy background of this decade, however, the Japanese in America felt somewhat at ease after the struggles with anti-Japanese nativists over the operation of language schools. The Supreme Court decision concerning a German language school teacher in Nebraska and Japanese-language schools in Hawaii (see chapters 7 and 3) allowed the Japanese immigrants to breathe again. In fact, Japanese-language schools were at their peak in the 1930s and functioned not only as language teaching institutions but also as community centers for local Japanese. However, for the majority of the Nisei, Japanese-language schools were a rather small part of their daily lives. The main focus was on life in local public schools as was the case with pupils of other immigrant groups at the time.

This chapter deals with the educational problems of the Nisei youths from 1927 until just before the outbreak of World War II. First, I will look briefly at the background of Nisei educational problems along with some statistical data. Second, I will touch on how U.S.-Japan relations during this period affected the Nisei as well as the Issei. Finally, I will examine the role that public school education and education in language schools played in the Japanese immigrant community.

Three Periods of Nisei Problems

In his discussion of the educational problem of the Nisei in Hawaii, Soen Yamashita categorized the educational problems into three distinctive periods.[1] The first period from 1892 through 1912 he refers to as the era of "Issei-oriented Nisei education." During this period, the Issei were mostly *dekasegi*-oriented. That is to say, they considered themselves sojourners rather than immigrants and dreamed of returning to their home villages with honor. Yamashita asserts that those Issei parents who were wealthy enough to afford to let their children move on to higher education did so only because the educated Nisei, having a good job upon their graduation, could help raise them from the bottom of the social ladder. Issei were busy thinking of their own lives without considering the education of the Nisei. Textbooks used in Japanese-language schools, including those for moral education, were compiled in Japan and authorized by the Mombusho.

The second period, according to Yamashita, lasted from 1913 until 1924, when the Immigration Law prohibited further immigration from Japan. Calling it the era of "Nisei education for the Nisei's sake," Yamashita maintains that it is in this period that the Issei began to recognize the problematic status of the Nisei and began looking for possible solutions. It is also during this period that Issei educators established educational policy in Japanese-language schools and became involved in the compilation of textbooks to replace those authorized by the Mombusho. He believes that the Issei gradually changed from seeing themselves as sojourners to seeing themselves as settlers on American soil.

The third period continues from 1925 until 1940, the time when Yamashita was writing. He concluded that the Nisei had become recognized as bona fide American citizens rather than the children of Japanese ancestry. Yamashita insists that the Nisei should always be good citizens of the United States but at the same time should be proud of the fact that they carry a strain of superior Japanese blood in their veins. Only by excelling as offspring of the Japanese race, he contends, can they contribute to American society and to the peace and prosperity of the Pacific. He goes on to say that although successes of the Nisei would not belong to Japanese nationals, their successes would be an honor and glory for the Japanese race at large.

One might argue that Yamashita's classification is based on the situation in Hawaii and that there were distinct differences in the circumstances of Japanese immigrants in Hawaii and in the continental United States. It is certainly true that the ratio of Japanese immigrants to the total population in Hawaii was significantly higher than the ratio on the mainland. In 1920, for instance, the number of Japanese was 109,274, or 43 percent of the total population in Hawaii.[2] Although 111,010 Japanese immigrants resided in the continental United States in the same year, the percentage of the total population there was minimal. The Japanese actually never comprised as much as 1 percent of the population in California, where more than half of the Japanese were concentrated. It should also be pointed out that by 1910 the number of Nisei over 15 years of age in Hawaii was approximately 20,000, comprising one-fourth of the total Japanese population there. In the same year, there were only 4,502 Nisei on the mainland. In fact, many of the Nisei citizens in Hawaii were older than the newly arrived Issei in Hawaii by 1910.[3] Considering this, the Nisei situation that Yamashita described in the second period (1912–1924) represents much of what went on in the third period (1924–1940) in California.

Given these differences and the limitations of his delineation of the Nisei problems, however, the social milieu of the Nisei and the changing attitudes of the Issei and Nisei were basically the same. In both regions, for example, there was a movement to outlaw all Japanese-language schools. The point here is not to try to compare circumstances surrounding Japanese immigrants in these two popular regions, but to use Yamashita's categorization as the background of the Nisei problem. Although the reality was not as simple as he contended, Yamashita's descriptions help us understand the Issei's perception of the education of the Nisei.

A Changing World and the Nisei

The number of newborn Nisei in California reached a peak in 1921, with over 5,000 newborns, and then steadily fell to a little over 1,500 in 1935, about the same figure as that for 1912.[4] Two factors contributed to this decline in the number of second-generation babies. First, the Japanese government stopped issuing passports to so-called "picture brides" in February 1920 out of fear of anti-Japanese sentiment among U.S. citizens. The second major factor for the decrease in Nisei births derived from the 1924 immigration law, which prohibited further Japanese immigration to the United States.

In the late 1920s, negative opinion of Japanese-language schools appeared to decrease. At least, that was what some Japanese leaders expressed in vernacular Japanese-American newspapers. They concluded that active exclusionists considered the exclusion law of 1924 to have settled the Japanese problem. Thus, overt discrimination against Japanese as shown in the activities of state lawmakers declined by the late 1920s. However, the Depression strongly affected the Japanese community and the Nisei in particular. The college-educated Nisei had to settle for whatever job they could find within their own ethnic community. Despite the optimistic opinions of the Issei leaders, covert discrimination continued. The Nisei could do nothing but accept the reality.

U.S.–Japan Relations and the Nisei as the Bridge of Understanding

The 1930s witnessed a new development in the Nisei's role in the Japanese community. As Jerrold Takahashi indicates, the late 1920s and 1930s were a period when the idea of a "cultural bridge" between the United States and Japan was formulated because of "the complex interplay of political and social ideologies of the time and from Japanese American responses to the social and racial attitudes of U.S. society."[5] Yuji Ichioka also points out, "Issei leaders originally formulated the concept that the Nisei should be nurtured to become a *Kusabi* or *Kakehashi*, a link or bridge of understanding between the United States and Japan."[6] And this concept was then tied to another concept, *Taiheiyo Jidai*, the Pacific Era. The bridge concept was first thought to be a "cultural bridge," but it gradually became more of a "political bridge" as years went by.

One of the most significant events in the early 1930s was the Manchurian Incident of September 1931. The Japanese Army in the South Manchuria Railway Zone stepped in to protect the railway on the pretense that Chinese troops had tried to blow it up. The fact of the matter was that a few high-ranking Japanese Army officials had plotted the explosion in order to establish a puppet regime. In March of the following year, Henry Pu-yi, former Emperor of China, assumed the position of Chief Executive of the new government in Manchuria.

Chinese residing in California vigorously protested the Japanese invasion of their homeland. On September 29 in Chinatown in San Francisco, hundreds of Chinese immigrants paraded through the streets and held a mass meeting in the Great China theater on Jackson Street.[7] A few Chinese stores removed Japanese goods from their shop windows. Finding themselves caught between the Issei's patriotism toward the Japanese government and condemnation by Chinese immigrants and American government, the Nisei felt helpless.

The Issei recognized that the majority of young Nisei were lacking enough knowledge of their parental homeland to be able to defend it. In response to the Nisei's reaction to the Manchurian Incident, the *Rafu Shimpo* published a special issue on the Sino-Japan situation in English under such headlines as "Japan's Position in Oriental Affairs," "Eternal Triangle of Chinese Military Leaders: Why China Is Not a Nation," and "South Manchurian Railway, Key to Prosperity."[8] The issue claimed that it was an attempt to help the public "face facts squarely" and "re-balance the rudimentary elements of the case."[9] It is not clear to what extent older Nisei showed interest in this issue. The incident provided the Issei with a chance to make the Nisei more aware of the Japanese situation, but it also put pressure on Nisei to justify Japan's position to the American public.

Japan's withdrawal from the League of Nations in 1933 isolated her from the rest of the world. The League of Nations adopted the Lytton Commission report and resolved that Manchuria would not be recognized as a nation and that the Japanese Army should pull out of Manchuria. Yosuke Matsuoka, who had studied at Oregon University and was the chief delegate of Japan to the League of Nations, declared that Japan would not yield to any proposal suggesting withdrawal from Manchuria. On his way back to Japan, Matsuoka stopped in the United States and received a warm welcome from the Japanese immigrants. Matsuoka visited San Francisco and delivered a lecture to an audience of 4,000 people. Touching upon problems in Manchuria and Japan's withdrawal from the League of Nations, he proceeded to talk about the Nisei. "The Nisei is the blood of the *Yamato* [Japanese] race implanted in America. They should make a pledge of allegiance to the United States while at the same time taking great pride in their ancestors. One hundred years from now, the people of America will recognize and appreciate that American citizens of Japanese blood in their vein [sic] play a major role in her culture."[10]

One can see how Matsuoka's speech parallels Yamashita's view on the Nisei. Both looked at the Nisei as Americans born and raised in America and felt they should contribute to the prosperity of American society. But they did not forget to remind the Nisei that the blood running in their veins was that of the "Yamato race," implying that Nisei are the offspring of what they considered the superior race.

The last five years of the prewar period witnessed full-fledged military conflict between China and Japan and the subsequent worsening of the relationship between Japan and the United States. What came to be known as the "2-26 Incident" of February 26, 1936, was a portent of the serious militarism that would lead to war. A coup attempt led by young army officers resulted in the killing of the Prime Minister and other leading political and military figures. Only a few opinions denouncing the coup attempt emerged, and Japan was certainly on the way to full-scale war against China. The Hirota Cabinet formed after the coup attempt played a crucial role in leading Japan toward war. The cabinet in August of that year adopted guidelines calling for turning some provinces of North China into Manchukuo areas.

What might have been a minor clash between Chinese and Japanese troops at the Marco Polo Bridge in the suburbs of Peking on July 7, 1937, escalated to a major battle between the two nations. The better-armed Japanese troops moved southward to Nanking. The imperial army, however, met Russian soldiers on the Manchurian borders and could no longer retreat from China. The Japanese people had become as intoxicated with early victories reported daily in newspapers as they had been in the previous wars with China in 1894 and Russia in 1905.

The Japan Times & Mail, an English newspaper company in Japan, published a booklet titled *The Truth Behind the Sino-Japanese Crisis: Japan Acts to Keep Eastern Civilization Safe for the World* in 1937. Contents included such articles as "Premier Fumimaro Konoye Defines Japan's Attitude," "Foreign Minister Koki Hirota on China Incident," "Chinese Deliberately Planned Hostilities, States Britisher," and "How China Compelled Japan to Act in Self-defense."[11] The booklet includes photos taken in China to justify the positions of the Japanese Army. Konoye Fumimaro, Premier of Japan, stated in his speech at Hibiya Public Hall, Tokyo, on September 11, 1937, as follows:

You already know that, on account of the lack of sincerity on the part of the Chinese, the Japanese government was forced to dispense with its previous policy of non-aggravation of the situation. The "North China Incident" has thus come to be termed "China Incident" instead. Now

*Japan is launching a positive and comprehensive-scaled punitive cam-
paign against the anti-Japanese elements in China.[12]*

Interpreting the incident as caused by the anti-Japanese elements
in China was a common view in vernacular Japanese-American newspapers in the United States. Although the true intention behind
publishing this booklet is not known, one can assume that Nisei
youths residing in Japan at that time had a chance to read it. If that
is the case, this publication might have been meant to inculcate the
Nisei with nationalistic sentiment toward Japan and further propa-
gate such ideas to Americans.

The Roosevelt administration expressed its objection to Japanese aggression in China in October 1937. In the summer of the
next year, the United States put an embargo on shipments of air-
craft, arms, and other war materials to Japan. Two years later, the
United States gave notice of intention to abrogate the nearly thirty-
year-old Treaty of Commerce and Navigation. In September 1940
the Japanese government signed a tripartite mutual defense pact with
Germany and Italy, which had a devastating effect on U.S.-Japan
relations.

Many disappointed Issei decided to leave the United States after the passage of 1924 Immigration Law, but those who stayed set
their minds on permanent settlement. Or perhaps it is more accurate to say that they decided not to return to Japan, whether or not
they were able to become citizens of the United States. However,
they never completely broke their ties with the homeland.

Maintaining affection and loyalty to the homeland is not necessarily a peculiar characteristic of Japanese immigrants. There are
numerous examples of organized activities among different immigrant groups to help their own homelands. Chinese immigrants
buying millions of dollars of Chinese war bonds to aid the defense
of China against Japan is one example. Another is German immigrants' attempts to demonstrate the German viewpoint to the general American public during World War I.[13]

The attachment to homeland is naturally stronger among first-
generation immigrants, who still hold an emotional attachment to
their native land. However, for American-born second-generation
children, loyalty to their ancestral land meant a dual or divided loy-

alty to two nations. Witnessing daily discrimination against their parents, some Nisei looked down on them while others felt pity, and still others tried to help them. Nisei had to face the complicated issue of loyalty. The majority of the Nisei in the continental United States in the 1920s, however, were too young to consider how they should behave as Americans of Japanese ancestry. In the 1930s, some of the Nisei who came of age started organizing their political voice as American citizens, though it was not until the late 1930s that their leadership in the community was solidified. For some, Americanism meant becoming 100 percent Americans with full allegiance to the United States of America. For others, the ghosts of their ancestors were always present, forcing them to pay back what they owed to their parents and their native land.

The China quagmire affected U.S.-Japan relations and the status of the Japanese immigrants. Adolescent Nisei in the late 1930s found it increasingly difficult to defend Japanese expansionism in China. Thousands of Nisei students who went to Japan to study began to return to the United States in the late 1930s. The Japanese American Citizens League (JACL), an organization of the Nisei established in 1931, expressed sympathy toward Japan but at the same time clearly took an American stance. They were in accord with the Issei's position in defending the actions taken by the Japanese government in 1931 and even up to 1937. However, beginning in late 1939 with the increasing possibility of war between the two nations, it became impossible for the JACL to defend the Japanese position. The Nisei were often accused of conducting fifth column activities. The American public's difficulty in distinguishing the American-born Japanese from the Japanese in Japan was part of the reason why the Nisei fell victim to such accusations. The JACL leaders, in an effort to publicize their patriotism to America, did not reject opportunities to cooperate with the FBI and other agencies in providing lists of Issei and Nisei disloyal to the United States. At the time of the relocation to the camps, they encouraged their fellow Japanese Americans to obey the order.

Nisei and Public School Education

If what Yamashita described is true, the sojourners from Japan who found their way to the territory of Hawaii or to the west coast of the continental United States around the turn of the century had little interest in the education of their own children. However, once they made up their minds to settle in the land of opportunity, they started thinking seriously about the education of their children.

Compared to other immigrants to America, the Japanese immigrants were on average well-educated. Those Japanese immigrants who arrived in the first two decades of the twentieth century were in fact among the best-educated immigrant groups. Over 90 percent of them were literate in Japanese, and on average, they had eight years of schooling, higher than the average for contemporary American adults.[14] Above all they seemed to believe that schooling for the children would be the major vehicle for their economic and social advancement. Therefore, it is natural to speculate that the Issei parents encouraged their children to work hard at public school.

In his study on public school education of Nisei in California, Reginald Bell concluded that there was little difference in intelligence levels between the Nisei student and the white American student.[15] The Nisei students excelled at all grade levels from the seventh through the twelfth and in all subjects. Bell attributed this scholastic achievement of Nisei to docility, industry, promptness, and home environment. Modell also states that a survey of 400 Los Angeles teachers in 1930 revealed that Nisei were not particularly exceptional; rather, their will to please and achieve was responsible for their academic success.[16]

Bell also touched on the academic achievement of Nisei in segregated public schools in Courtland, Florin, Isleton, and Walnut Grove. Compared to Nisei students in public schools where the Japanese population was not dominant, there was a slight educational underachievement. He speculated that the lack of interaction with native English-speaking fellow pupils prevented the students from acquiring the appropriate English language skills and, therefore, limited general scholastic achievement. He also studied the effect of Japanese-language schools and found no advantage to accrue on educational tests to either attendants or nonattendants of the language school. Thus he concluded that the effect of attendance at Japanese-language schools on overall educational achievement was negligible.[17]

The Issei had high expectations for public school education and were eager to see high scholastic achievement among the Nisei. Local vernacular newspapers repeatedly reported that the Issei parents were content with the Nisei's excellence in public schools. They considered Nisei achievements to be not only individual but also collective accomplishments of the Japanese immigrants as a whole. The public schools, therefore, helped the Issei maintain their self-esteem through satisfaction and pride in their offspring. Unfortunately, however, no matter how much the Nisei achieved in school, schooling did not provide economic opportunity for them. Actually, the schools were irrelevant to economic and social advancement. Nisei males by 1940 were mostly dependent on Issei enterprise, most of which had to do with farming. Both Issei and Nisei felt that the best vocational possibility for a Nisei was to work for a big Japanese firm. However, despite the plea of the Central Japanese Association to the Japanese government, no particular effort and arrangement for the Nisei seemed to have been made. For Nisei females, too, the job situation was quite bleak.[18]

Although Issei parents found cultural value, if not economic advancement, in American public school education, they were not always satisfied with the way their children were taught in school. Perhaps because of their great faith in the value of public education, their confidence in it often eroded. Compared to the stringent education they had received at public schools in Japan, they found schooling in America too relaxed and easy-going. Both the absence of "examination hell" and the fewer school days were sources of complaint. In the late 1930s, the average school days per year in California was 178 days as opposed to 220 days in Japan.[19] Dissatisfied parents blamed the easiness of the schools for the Nisei's lack of discipline.

In fact, without touching on the moral and spiritual foundation on which Issei parents stood, one cannot discuss overall education for the Nisei. The kind of education Issei parents received in their childhood determined their attitude toward the Nisei to a great degree. Thus, let us briefly look at the Isseis' educational background.

When the Meiji government enacted *Gakusei* (the educational system) in 1872, textbooks used for moral education classes were practically all translations of Western publications, especially in French and English. The Western principles in these textbooks were freedom and democracy. The people, used to the hierarchical relationships between ruler and ruled, could not adjust to the sudden changes. Reflecting a reactionary movement against Westernization in the second and third decades of the Meiji period, moral education returned to the previous *chu* (loyalty) and *ko* (filial piety) orientation of Confucianism. This emphasis on the importance of the cultivation of morals within formal education was further intensified by the rise of nationalism in the late 1890s when Japan warred with China. The state was considered to be an extension of the family. Thus every family member was expected to obey the head of the family, in this case, the emperor.

By 1880, the Meiji government prohibited most moral education textbooks that were translations of Western materials. At the same time, the government decided to make *Shushin* (moral education) an absolute priority in order to inculcate Confucian morality. The Minister of Education, Arinori Mori, was determined to fully utilize education for the benefit of *Fukoku Kyohei* (wealth and military strength). He insisted that even at the national university the main emphasis should be on the state, not academics. Although Mori was assassinated before enactment of the Imperial Rescript on Education in 1890, his ideas were well represented in the Imperial Rescript.[20]

In February 1880, at a meeting of local chief government officials, a discussion took place regarding the chaotic state of moral education created by the introduction of Western democracy and individualism. These officials decided to ask the Cabinet for a national policy on moral education. Then the Minister of Education, Takeaki Enomoto, argued that the Japanese should adopt Confucianism as their standard. The Imperial Rescript, drafted by Kowashi Inoue and Eifu Motoda, stressed the historical significance and glory of Japan as a nation, founded by an ancestor of the emperor, and urged that all subjects sacrifice everything for the sake of protecting the emperor's land from outsiders.

Inoue Tetsujiro, in his manual on the Imperial Rescript, *Chokugo Engi* (1890), stressed that what the emperor is to his subjects is what parents are to their children: the nation is an extension of family. Moral education based upon the Imperial Rescript continued for more than a half a century, from 1890 until the Japanese surrender in 1945. Thus it is important to note that the Issei received this moralistic education when they were in Japan as students, although there is no way of knowing how seriously each Issei took such instruction.

Akiyoshi Hayashi, in his study on Japanese moral instruction in Japanese-language schools in prewar Hawaii, states that greater emphasis was placed on aristocratic traits than on democratic traits in moral instruction. He further suggests that the moral instruction "help[ed] keep the Japanese children within the fold of the family and encourage[d] sympathetic understanding and appreciation of the ideals of their parents."[21] Although Japanese influence was stronger in Hawaii than in California, the fundamental philosophy of the Issei was the same in both states. Issei expected Japanese-language schools to play a role in transmitting the cultural heritage of the *Yamato Minzoku* (the Japanese race) rather than simply teaching the Japanese language. Those Issei who were not satisfied with their children's progress in Japanese-language skills had a better option, namely, sending the children to Japan for study.

While the parents had high hopes of the second-generation becoming the "bridge of understanding," they felt that their children were falling into indolent habits. Frustrated at the difficulties of controlling their own children, the Issei looked for help to the Japanese-language school. The higher the expectations of the Japanese-language school became, the more frustration it caused the parents. The school itself was precluded from effectively functioning as a language and moral instruction institution due to the limited instructional hours and lack of motivation on the part of the students, among other reasons.

A "Bridge of Understanding" and Japanese-Language Schools

Ethnic mother-tongue schools were not special features of the Japanese community alone. Most ethnic groups established their own mother-tongue schools, and some ethnic communities were even successful in making public schools modify curricula to the extent that they could accommodate teaching in their mother-tongue. The Germans, especially in the Midwest, made German a regular part of the public school curriculum. In California during the mid-nineteenth century, a substantial number of Spanish-speaking children were taught in their mother tongue. Scandinavians, Italians, Czechs, Dutch, and other European groups demanded public schools to allow their language as a part of the school curriculum. There also existed Catholic parochial schools, a full-fledged school system.[22]

The main significance of learning Japanese was, at least for some Issei intellectuals and leaders, to achieve the goal of *Tozai Bunka Yugo* or the harmonization of Eastern and the Western cultures. Some Issei openly showed their nationalistic sentiment to Japan, and insisting on the superiority of the Japanese, they forced the Nisei to learn the Japanese language. Others believed that the significance of teaching Japanese to the Nisei lay in the promotion of their ethnic pride. Proponents of this idea thought that all the good aspects of Japan—her culture, arts, literature, religion, values, and customs—should not be confined to the small islands of Japan. Nisei should inherit Japanese traditions and plant them on American soil. Japanese Consul-General Kaname Wakasugi, in his New Year message in 1932, averred that the Nisei youth should utilize their cultural and linguistic heritage to make themselves useful in the new era of the Pacific:

[Y]our ancestral country, Japan, has maintained and cultivated the moral standard of the Orient which has stood the test of time for several thousands of years. . . . Therefore, if the second-generation Japanese would study and acquire the knowledge of the Japanese language through which they can learn of the life and thought of the Japanese people, they will be in an excellent position to be able to absorb most advantageously into their American life the essence of the highest qualities of the Orient. . . . Today, with the dawn of a New Age, the theatre of the world's activities which had hereto been centered on the European stage, is now gradually and steadily shifting toward the Pacific. The rising generation will surely live to see the New Era of the Pacific grow into the brighter light of the day, so that the East and the West will meet in a better and close understanding.[23]

The Consul's optimistic and idealistic observations represent the view of most immigrant intellectuals in this period. They hoped that the new generation would do something constructive for both the United States and Japan at the dawn of the Pacific Era. For that to happen, Nisei should be bicultural and bilingual, an extremely difficult assignment for the majority of them. Born as citizens of the

United States and educated in public schools, the Nisei acquired American culture and spoke English as native speakers. Yet the fact that they were born to Japanese parents and raised by them did not automatically guarantee that they had acquired Japanese culture and were fluent in Japanese. With the exception of a few Nisei who sincerely attempted to achieve the mission, the majority of the Nisei took it as mere idealism.

As the Japanese military involvement in Asia continued, the two generations again found a gap existed between them. Issei expectations became a burden for some Nisei. For the Issei who expected their children to become defenders of Japan at the outbreak of the China Incident in 1937, the Nisei's reaction was indeed very disappointing. The majority of Nisei were rather indifferent to the incident and remained detached observers.

The Japanese Language School Associations continued their policy of Beishu Nichiju (primary emphasis on America and secondary emphasis on Japan) in the early 1930s. However, this general principle was not clearly expressed in individual schools. At Suisun Hogo Gakko in Suisun, Solano County, California, for example, the Japanese Association and the school administrators were not definite about the educational policy of the school at a meeting held in January 1933. Some insisted on purely Japanese-style education based on the Imperial Rescript of Education, while others proposed a more American orientation. As was the case at many other meetings in the immigrant community, they were not able to reach a resolution. Considering that the 1927 ruling emancipated Japanese-language schools from legal restrictions, some schools might well have shifted their educational policy more toward the Nisshu Beiju (primary emphasis on Japan and secondary emphasis on America).

On the other hand, some Issei intellectuals felt serious doubt about an excessive emphasis on the moral aspects of Japanese education. An editorial in the *Nichi Bei Shimbun* in 1929 severely criticized the failure of moral education in Japan. The editorial stated:

Despite the extraordinary emphasis on shushin dotoku *or moral education in the Japanese educational system, it has had very little effect on the Japanese people. If such an education were an effective one, Japan should have become a land of gentlemen. The reality is totally the opposite. The more the moral teaching is indoctrinated upon the people, the worse they seem to become in character . . . The main point of education is to cultivate one's reflective thought. Men usually do not become immoral as long as they possess reflective consciousness. And thus they do not need the extraordinary moral lessons. Reflecting upon this point, we should be particularly happy and grateful about the unfettered education the Nisei has received in America.*[24]

The first-prize essay given in the New Year's essay contest by the *Nichi Bei Shimbun* in 1936 referred to the difficulty of transferring the Japanese style of education to the Japanese-language school in the United States: "There are many people these days who wish to combine the aim of teaching the Japanese with that of cultivating the Japanese spirit. Yet the Japanese spirit will never be mastered by those who live outside of Japan."[25] The author further stated that it would be difficult to teach what the Japanese spirit really means even to those living in Japan and thus it would be close to impossible to implant such a difficult notion of Japanese spirit into the Nisei through the Japanese language and Japanese history. It is interesting to find that the essay denouncing the teaching of the Japanese spirit received the first prize from the vernacular newspaper most widely read among the Japanese in the United States.

A number of Japanese immigrant newspaper articles reported the majority of the Issei in Japanese communities in the 1930s were preoccupied with Japanese military activities in China, as discussed earlier. In every Japanese community, movie shows and lectures on the Japanese army's activities in China were routinely given for the Issei. Japanese-language schools were often chosen as the place for these events. Although the films and lectures were mainly designed for the Issei, they were also seen by Nisei youngsters.

Yet again, we do not know how seriously these events were taken by the Nisei pupils. The average age of the Nisei in 1933 was 12, and they comprised approximately 40 percent of the Japanese immigrants.[26] One anecdote put it that one Nisei child told his parents that if he hit a home run in Japan, the ball would fall into the sea. The symbolic size of the land of Japan was expanding in the mind of the Issei, yet somehow contracting in the mind of the young Nisei.

It was common practice for the Japanese immigrants, as was the case with most of the immigrants communities in America, to send materials and money to their homeland for the purpose of helping those suffering from natural disasters such as catastrophic earthquakes. This practice also applied to helping Japanese soldiers in China and soldiers' families. Charity events were held in several Japanese communities. Shows often dealt with war-related themes, which conjured up patriotic sentiment toward Japan. Different Japanese immigrant organizations collected money and took it to the Japanese consulate, which in turn sent it to Japan. In Japanese-language schools, too, pupils were involved in this custom called *Imonkin,* comfort money. One hundred ninety-one pupils of Marysville Gakuen in Marysville, Yuba County, California, for instance, saved their pocket money and sent a total of 100 yen to Japan in order to help the bereaved.[27]

Japanese-language speech contests were frequently held for young members of the Japanese communities. One writer in *Nichi Bei Shimbun* analyzed the rise and fall of speech contests in Fresno between 1927 and 1933.[28] The first two years were a slump period because the *Yobiyose* (summoned Japan-born youth) had already reached maturity and the Nisei were still too young. By 1930, the contestants were all U.S.-born Nisei. During the final two years of his analysis, the number of Nisei who reached adolescence had increased. These Nisei felt compelled to try to master the Japanese language.

English speech contests were also common events for the Nisei. Ida Shimanouchi was the winner of an oratorical contest at the Kinmon Gakuen auditorium in San Francisco in May 1933. In her speech, she insisted that the future of the Pacific was with the Nisei, stating: "Upon them [Nisei] lie the solution to the development of the great peaceful future of the Pacific."[29] She also believed that if the Nisei youth were strong enough to face the problem and wise enough to meet future problems, there would be no more misunderstandings between the United States and Japan. The tone of the speech was typical of those Nisei adolescents who wished to serve as a "bridge of understanding" between the United States and Japan in what they perceived to be the coming Pacific Era. Indeed, it may not be an exaggeration to say that the very reason that speech contests in both English and Japanese were so frequently held lay in the Issei's expectation that the Nisei should actively play such a role. Generally, however, if Nisei youngsters could find any rewards in acquiring the Japanese-language skills, they found them in a more practical way.

Mushrooming Growth of Japanese-Language Schools

The *Nichi Bei Shimbun* in October 1928 editorialized that Japanese in California showed a change of attitude from that of a sojourner mentality to a more permanent outlook. This editorial congratulated Issei for finally deciding to make America their home and stated that the main reason behind this change of mind was the maturation of the Nisei. The editorial also referred to the prominent increase of Japanese-language schools. The writers felt that they could hardly find anyone who opposed the teaching of the Japanese language to the Nisei and that America itself would expect Nisei to acquire the language skills to become a tie to bind the United States and Japan. They also strongly felt that Japanese-language schools had come to be the center of the Japanese community. In practical terms, the school building was often used as a meeting place for the parent associations and youth groups. In their eyes, Japanese-language schools were replacing functions once played by local Japanese Associations.[30]

The *Rafu Shimpo* in Los Angeles in 1932 also pointed out the increasing number of Japanese schools in southern California:

There are more than 120 Japanese-language schools in Southern California, clustering around Los Angeles. If small schools like "shijuku," or private class at one's home, of five to ten children, were added, the number will reach 150. The Japanese-language school has become truly a fashion these days. The enrollment figure is approximately 8,200 and teachers number over 200. Considering the days when people argued the significance of establishing these language schools, I feel I am living in quite a different age.[31]

Zaibei Nihonjin-shi, published in 1940, revealed that there were 134 such schools in northern and central California and 126 in southern California. The comparison of these two groups is of interest. In terms of years of establishment, the former created 20 schools in the period 1903–1912, 73 in 1913–1927, and 39 in the period 1928–1941, while the latter founded 3, 57, and 47 in the respective periods. The "boom" period was, interestingly enough, between 1913 and 1927, a time filled with Americanization pressures and legal restrictions. As observed in a previous chapter, the number of new-born Nisei peaked in California in 1921, which indicates that the number of school-age children started decreasing in 1927. Therefore, the decrease in the establishment of Japanese-language schools corresponds with the diminishing pool of school-age Nisei children.[32]

Differences between the northern/central California and southern California schools can be found related to at least the following two points. The year of establishment is older for the former group, showing 20 schools in the period 1903–1912, with only 3 schools in the latter group. On the contrary, at least 47 schools were created in southern California during 1927–1941, whereas 39 new schools were founded in northern/central California. Another difference is that southern California schools tended to name themselves more freely than their counterparts in northern/central California. The large number of schools in northern/central California were named according to their locations, mostly the names of streets or towns. Many southern California schools used personal names (Onodera, Wazu, Fuji, Midori, etc.), names of churches (Mii Kyokai, Mariner, San Diego Bukkyokai, etc.), and even names of associations (Sanko Nihojin Kumiai Kyokai). One possible explanation is that schools in southern California were mostly established after the most intense anti-Japanese sentiment had subsided, that is, post–1924 (immigration law) and post–1927 (foreign language school control laws), allowing the immigrant group to express their Japanese identity more freely.

Edward Strong claims that by the early 1930s approximately 69 percent of the Nisei in California attended Japanese-language schools for an average of three years.[33] According to R.W. O'Brien, however, attendance in language schools varied in different communities; 95 percent of the Nisei in four segregated public schools in central California enrolled in Japanese-language schools while in urban Seattle only 29 percent of the Nisei attended language schools.[34]

The growing number of language schools in some areas indeed

caused competition in attracting students. In Boyle Heights, Los Angeles, for example, there were four schools within a few blocks. One female student, when reproached by the teacher, told him that she did not have to come to his school.[35] This stiff competition caused people to call for the amalgamation of small schools. Merging these schools was strongly advocated by community leaders in order to improve facilities and efficiency of instruction. These schools were just like private elementary schools in the Edo period in Japan called *terakoya*, they observed—with similar expenditures:

The total expenditures of all these Japanese-language schools are close to $300,000 dollars. Parents have to cover all the expenses for tuition and other school-related costs. Particularly, parents of small schools face a large expenditure. Several schools in one small section experience stiff competition. When one school purchased a newly modeled school bus, then the other schools followed and tried to buy better buses. The financial burdens for the parents keep accumulating in this way.[36]

Tsutae Sato enumerated advantages of centralized schools and disadvantages of numerous small decentralized schools. Advantages of centralized schools include: (1) the teacher need only teach one grade; (2) the teacher can instruct the pupils at the same level; (3) the individual aptitude of the pupil is respected; (4) the study of instructional materials can be furthered; and (5) school facilities will be improved. With regard to the disadvantages of decentralized schools, he referred to the following: (1) the teacher needs to teach pupils of different grades simultaneously; (2) the teacher instructs the pupil indirectly; (3) the pupil tends to waste time without knowing what to do; (4) the study of instructional materials tends to be done sporadically; (5) teaching plans are often carelessly prepared; and (6) school facilities are inadequate.[37] Schools were established by parents of different interests and background. Thus, it was not easy to unify several schools to create one centralized school. It was almost impossible to do so when there were different religiously affiliated schools in one community. The commute of the pupils was another problem for the establishment of the centralized school. While it was pedagogically ideal to create centralized schools, many obstacles prevented small schools from unification.

Teachers

It was not uncommon for the average Japanese to attend universities in Japan before the 1930s. During the period between 1910 and 1930 there had been a rapid expansion in the area of higher education in Japan. The number of universities increased from three to forty-six during these twenty years, with the number of graduates rising from 8,392 in 1910 to 35,630 in 1920. The rapid growth of highly educated graduates far exceeded the demand in the workplace. In 1929, only 38.1 per cent of the graduates in law, literature, and economics found jobs.[38]

A survey of Japanese-language schools in the Northern California area by the Japanese Consulate includes material on the educational backgrounds of each of the teachers working at every school surveyed. One of the most prominent characteristics of these teachers is that their educational backgrounds are relatively high. A good number of teachers had attended universities in the United States, and of the 256 teachers in the survey, almost one fourth of them graduated from universities in Japan.

A distinctive element in the educational backgrounds of a number of these teachers is that many of them had graduated from Buddhist universities in Japan, particularly Ryukoku Daigaku in Kyoto, a Buddhist university. About 25 teachers graduated from this institution out of the total of 256 teachers surveyed.[39] These teachers taught not only at Buddhist Japanese-language schools but also at other schools with no religious affiliation. One possible reason for this number of Ryukoku graduates may be that people who were classified as ministers of religion could enter the United States much more easily than other Japanese immigrants.

Becoming a teacher at a Japanese-language school was not easy in the early 1930s. The Depression affected every corner of society. Forty people applied for one teaching position at a Japanese-language school in a rural area of San Diego County in the early 1930s, and the competition was even more severe at urban schools, where applicants could find universities they wanted to attend.[40] Still, teachers may have wondered if they were fortunate, after all, to get the jobs. In areas such as Boyle Heights in Los Angeles where many Japanese language schools existed, teachers had to struggle to recruit pupils for their schools.

Pupils were too tired to study after the regular public school day, and there were few rewards for learning the language in terms of receiving credits toward advancement to higher institutions of learning. Teachers commonly faced pupils who could not read even half the *kanji* (Chinese characters) in a lesson. Some teachers were frustrated and did not know what to do, although others continually sought better ways of motivating their students.

Teaching, though oftentimes frustrating and lowly ranked in American society, could of course still be a rewarding experience. Yusen Kawamura, a prolific writer and an editor of a textbook on the Japanese language, reflected upon his ten years of teaching experience as he was about to return to Japan. He recalls, "The happiest occasion that I always remember is the time when I met my former students jumping at me with smiling faces, saying, 'Sensei' (Teacher). Those pupils whom I scolded more often are unforgettable. Once in a while I encounter great satisfaction when these former students politely greet me in proper Japanese."[41]

Kawamura taught in schools in Watsonville, New Castle, and Filton. Kawamura's experiences as a Japanese-language school teacher remind us of the danger in making sweeping generalizations about teachers in Japanese-language schools. Clearly, the Japanese-language school provided him with some rewards—social status as a teacher in various Japanese communities, a moderate but sufficient salary for living, and a great deal of psychological satisfaction through integration with community members and school children. A Japanese-language school teacher in Washington shared this satisfied feeling by saying, "Though we educators were not materially rewarded, we were often fully content and felt a joy which goes beyond material thing[s]."[42]

The concerns of teachers were manifold. However, the biggest frustration that they faced was the limited time for instruction. In practice it was sometimes difficult for pupils to find a Japanese-language school within walking distance, unless they lived in a heavily Japanese area. Therefore, attendance could be irregular.

Kawamura said at one point that most of a teacher's energy was used in efforts to please parents rather than teach the language to students. In one school, twelve teachers left in ten years; ten were dismissed by parents and two quit on their own. Indeed, teachers in public schools sometimes experienced similar pressures. However, supported by a relatively small number of parents, Japanese-language school teachers could never possess as much autonomy as public school teachers. Under such adverse circumstances, more and more teachers felt discouraged about teaching at Japanese-language schools by the middle to late 1930s.[43] The lack of rewards (perceived and otherwise) resulted in a decreasing number of qualifying teachers.

Teachers occasionally assembled together to improve their teaching skills by exchanging information and hearing lectures. Teachers in Redwood, Menlo Park, Mountainview, Palo Alto, Mayfield, and Los Altos established what they called a "folk college" in order to enhance their knowledge of philosophy, history, sociology, politics, and current affairs as well as education. They met once a month to hear lectures. A similar learning group of teachers formed in Southern California, informally gathering to create haiku poems and to practice a chorus for the Los Angeles Olympics.[44] At Rafu Dai-ni Gakuen, there was a haiku poets' circle called "Olive Ginsha," where teachers and parents created and shared haiku poems. Some of the representative haiku poets in California were among members of this group.[45]

On February 11, 1940, Japan celebrated the 2,600th anniversary of its founding, and Japanese communities in California observed the event. In Los Angeles, for example, traditional ceremonies took place at the Yamato Hall with the participation of over 150 Japanese language school pupils.[46] The *Rafu Shimpo* published an anniversary volume containing a historical sketch of Japanese imperial history (in both English and Japanese), numerous pictures of the immigrant community, and personality sketches of important figures in the community. At the end of the abridged English translation of the survey of 26 centuries of Japanese history, a Nisei salute to the anniversary was added. The salute read:

On the 2600th anniversary celebration of the founding of Nippon, we bow in reverence to the past, in prayer to the future. And to those of us who are American citizens [N]isei on these shores of the Pacific, there is both thankfulness born out of an appreciation for the heritage of Nippon and a pride in the newer traditions of our homeland— America.[47]

While appreciating their heritage as Japanese, they did not forget to mention that their homeland is America, not Japan. In fact, in the message, it is repeatedly emphasized that America is the Nisei's home.

To bring a fuller and deeper understanding between the peoples of two neighboring countries, the [N]isei must make firm root and permanence on the soil they know as home—America. The [N]isei must become part and parcel imbedded in the life of America, for only by so doing will they secure acceptance of their racial background by their fellow American citizens and neighbors.[48]

Included were compositions of the students at various Japanese-language schools in honor of the special occasion. Interestingly enough, the contents of many of the 39 compositions are in many ways identical. Beginning with a mention that 2,600 years have passed since Jinmu Tenno (Emperor Jinmu) ascended the throne in Kashihara Shrine in Yamato, the compositions praise the unbroken line of sovereign emperors and the people's continuous loyalty to them. They go on to refer to the fact that Japan has never experienced a defeat in any war with foreign countries—the Mongolian Invasions of 1274 and 1281, the Sino-Japanese War of 1894–5, and the Russo-Japanese War of 1904–5. The unity of the Emperor and his subjects are attributed to this achievement. The 1937 Sino-Japanese conflict is also discussed as a holy war aimed at the establishment of peace in the East. Acknowledging that the situation has been interpreted otherwise by Americans, the essays emphasize that it is the Nisei who can explain and remove misleading notions about Japan then circulating among the American people. The compositions end with the students' determination to become a tie binding and promoting friendly relations between the United States and Japan.

Given the near identical content and choice of words in the compositions, it is rather obvious that many of the compositions were either edited or possibly even written by school teachers or other Issei editors. Or perhaps, compositions were modeled after one composition distributed to students. Some essays nonetheless reflected what was going on inside classrooms and the immigrant community in 1940:

I can hear my Japanese neighbor playing the 2,600th anniversary record today, too. At the Japanese-language school that I have been going to, I sing a song about the 2,600th anniversary and listen to the teacher explaining about the event. The 2,600th year is deeply impressed in the minds of the Japanese people. I might as well say "The year 2600!" instead of greeting "Ohayo gozaimasu" (Good morning). In my house, there is a scroll hanging on the wall written by my father on the New Year's Day, saying "The 2,600th Year of the Imperial Reign." Every time I see it, I feel proud to be Japanese.[49]

We need to be cautious about describing what went on inside classrooms. Some teachers may have self-identified as patriotic Japanese subjects, while others may have stood vehemently against Japanese militaristic involvement in China, hoping for a peaceful conclusion. It is easy to imagine that in the minds of many teachers there was fear that one day Japan might fight with the United States.

Chapter Five
The Bridge of Understanding over the Pacific
The Nisei in Japan

"Aa natsukashi no fubo no kuni . . .[Oh, beloved land of my parents . . .]"

—Nanka Hihongo Gakuen Kyokai
Kengaku Ryoko Nisshi Kinencho (1939)

In the mid-1930s, although racial conflict still existed, anti-Japanese sentiment did not bother the Japanese immigrants as much as it did in the previous decade. Once external pressure was on the decrease, their attention shifted more to a domestic problem—the education of their children. This does not mean that the problem had not existed earlier. It is perhaps more accurate to say that for the first time since settling, Japanese immigrants had the luxury of taking their children's education seriously. In the mid-1930s, the average age of the Issei in the continental United States was approximately 50 years. And there was an increasing number of Nisei who came of age.

There were two choices available to the Issei parents for the education of their children. One was to raise them in the United States; the other was to send them to Japan. Many Issei parents chose the latter by sending their children to Japan where their relatives were asked to take care of them. The majority of such Nisei children were found in such *Iminken,* prefectures with a high percentage of emigrants, such as Hiroshima, Yamaguchi, and Fukuoka.

The Foreign Affairs Ministry conducted a survey regarding the number of Nisei residents in Japan in 1933. According to the survey, there were 11,317 in Hiroshima, 2,301 in Yamaguchi, 1,769 in Fukuoka, 1,534 in Wakayama, and 1,480 in Okayama prefectures.

Taking a closer look at Hiroshima, we find that while 3,920 Nisei were 15 years old and over, 7,397 were younger than 15 years old, indicating that 65 percent of those in Hiroshima had not reached high school age. In terms of their homeland, 54 percent were from the mainland United States while the rest were from Hawaii.[1]

When these younger Nisei returned to the United States after reaching their adolescence, they were called Kibei (returnees), and tended to form a separate group from the rest of the Nisei who were born and raised in the United States. Harry Kitano introduces Leighton's study which estimates that over 9 percent in one of the evacuation camps were Kibei. Kitano regards this figure as a typical distribution, and thus a group of significant size. He also states that the practice of sending at least one child back to Japan for educational purposes was most common between 1920 and 1940, a period during which rampant nationalism and patriotism were prevalent in Japan. Thus, many of the Kibei returned to the United States with strong pro-Japanese feeling, which resulted in inevitable conflict with other Nisei.[2]

The number of Nisei in the United States was only 4,502 in 1910 but rapidly increased more than sixfold to 29,672 in 1920. Without restrictive measures, the Nisei population might have increased in the mainland United States. However, in the 1920s several legal and diplomatic actions were taken to prevent a further influx of Japanese immigrants. The Department of State, for example, sent a letter on November 22, 1919, to Katsuji Debuchi, Counsellor of the Japanese Embassy, saying that the rapid increase in the numbers of "picture brides" threatened a continuance of the problems which had supposedly been settled by the Gentlemen's Agreement of 1908. It also provided figures of male and female Japanese immigrants admitted at mainland ports during the years 1902–1908 and 1909–1919. While the total numbers of male and female immigrants during the period 1902–1908 was 45,415 and 5,925 respectively, those in the period from 1909 to 1919 revealed that there were only 23,133 males whereas the number of females jumped to 28,237.[3] Responding to this request from the U.S. government, its Japanese counterpart decided to cease the issuance of passports to "picture brides" in February 1920.

The major blow to Japanese immigrants, however, came in the spring of 1924, when the U.S. Congress passed the Immigration

Act of 1924. This act, which became effective on July 1, 1924, in practice nullified the Gentlemen's Agreement of 1908 by prohibiting the admission of those Japanese ineligible for citizenship. Section 13 (c) of the Act states that "no alien ineligible to citizenship shall be admitted to the United States" unless otherwise stated. The passage of this act automatically meant that the growth of the Japanese community in the United States would be restricted in the coming years. Along with the years of internment during the World War II period, the year 1924 had an unforgettable impact on the minds of the Japanese immigrants. From 1921 to 1929, the number of the Japanese nationals who left American shores surpassed those who arrived, resulting in a total decrease in the Japanese population in the United States of 14,148.[4] Naturally, the rate of increase among the Nisei population also declined sharply. Nonetheless, by 1930 the Nisei amounted to more than half of the contemporary Japanese population of approximately 140,000 in the mainland United States.

Accompanying those Issei who returned to Japan, Nisei children saw their ancestral hometown and villages for the first time in their lives. In addition to these youngsters, there were Nisei youths who visited Japan as tourists.

Visiting Japan

Beginning in the mid-1920s, *Kengakudan,* tours to Japan, were popular events not only for the Nisei but also for the Issei. Sponsored by local vernacular newspaper companies, *Kenjinkai* (prefectural associations), youth groups (i.e., Nanka Seinen Domei, or the Southern California Youth League), and others, groups of Japanese immigrants both young and old organized trips to Japan for various purposes.

In 1924, four Nisei girls were sent to Japan by the Seattle Japanese Association. There was a definite purpose behind their visit to Japan. As various Nisei had grown older and become junior high and high school students, they compared their parents' standard of living and social status with those of white parents. These young Nisei tended to believe that their parents were destined to be discriminated against because of their lower standard of living and unsophisticated behavior. While fully acknowledging that they were the children of the oppressed, they could not help feeling disdain for their parents' unrefined behavior and the land that produced them.

The Issei, on the other hand, sincerely hoped that some day their children would take pride in the strain of Yamato or Japanese blood in their veins. Respect for their Japanese blood was the essential ingredient required for becoming "a bridge of understanding" between the two nations. The Issei in Seattle concluded that the best way to fill the gap between the ideal and reality would be to send representative Nisei students to Japan and have them observe the true state of affairs.

The four representative female Nisei were at first reluctant to accept the mission to the land of their roots. However, they did go to Japan and as they came in touch with real people and the circumstances surrounding them, the previously held aversion and misgivings about their ancestral land gave way to positive sentiments. The Issei organizer was very happy with the outcome. The Nisei female students conducted a series of lecture trips to other Japanese communities on the mainland to report on their experiences and received a warm welcome in every Japanese community they visited.[5]

In the 1930s, Japanese communities sent their Nisei youths not only to Japan but also to its colonies. When the Southern California Japanese Language School Association arranged their second *Kengakudan* tour in 1939, the members spent two months visiting such places as Tokyo, Nagoya, Kyoto, Nara, Osaka, Okayama, Hiroshima, Hakata, Kumamoto, and Kagoshima, many of which were hometowns of their parents. In Tokyo, they had opportunities to meet their Imperial Highnesses the Prince and Princess Chichibu and a number of notable civilian and military figures. After visiting these places in Japan from July 8 to July 15, the tour group embarked on a steamer at Shimonoseki headed for Pusan, Korea. After arriving in Korea, they proceeded further north and found themselves busily sightseeing in Keijo, Hsinking, Harbin, Fushun, and Mukden. They even went southwest to Peking and Tientsin in China before they finally returned to Moji port in Japan on August 15.

Led by Endo Koshiro, principal of Compton Gakuen, a Japanese language school in Los Angeles, and three other conductors, thirty-four members and nine semi-members participated in this tour. The list of conductors and members of the *Kengakudan* shows their ancestral prefectures. The most widely represented prefecture was Kumamoto with 12 members; followed by Fukuoka six;

Kanagawa and Hiroshima five; Miyagi four; and Yamaguchi, To-kyo, Niigata, and Okayama with two each. Others included such prefectures as Fukushima, Saitama, and Yamanashi. These numbers do not necessarily match the configuration of the representative prefectures of the Japanese immigrants in the States. Yet, they roughly mirror the so-called *Iminken.*

Reading impressions of the tour written by the participants, one can find the following shared comments. First, they were impressed with the "miniature natural beauty" and the abundance of temples and shrines in Japan. As they occasionally witnessed the Japanese humbly bowing their heads at these sacred places, they felt the religiousness of the Japanese. Some of them tried to associate the faithfulness with *Yamato-damashii,* of which they were repeatedly told back in the United States. One student commented, "I have often heard that Japan was 'kami-no-kuni' (God's country)." He concluded that that was true when he found numerous temples and shrines and the people offering daily prayers.

Second, the members were often puzzled by contrasts—the old and the new Japan, the past and present coexisting everywhere they visited. Contemporary buildings and modern conveniences in Tokyo were no different from those on Fifth Avenue in New York. Department stores as modern and novel as those on Broadway stood along the main avenues. But the busy streets were also filled with street vendors equipped only with canvas roofs, selling merchandise side by side. While modern concrete buildings complete with heating and cooling systems made the city look quite contemporary, wooden houses with tile roofs on the outskirts of the city manifested the old and traditional aspect of Japan. Trains were big and comfortable and ran on time, even ahead of schedule sometimes. But the travelers did not fail to see *jinrickshas* scuttling across the town.

Third, the participants felt that they could not have had a kinder reception than they experienced in Japan. In every city they visited, they were given a hearty welcome with lavish banquets. Even taking their stories with a grain of salt, one can easily assume that the majority of the Nisei tourists had never experienced such hospitality back in the United States. They were often amazed at the quality and quantity of courtesy everywhere they visited. The announcements by uniformed bus attendants were funny even for them. "We are now coming to a corner, please be careful—," "We have arrived at xx hotel, please see that you do not leave anything behind." Many Nisei must have a hard time restraining themselves when confronted by such excessive consideration.

Last, but not least, the Nisei in the tour could not help noticing nationalistic sentiment in Japan. They saw people cheering soldiers with banners and flags at stations. In the countryside, they found few men, but rather women and young girls working hard under the scorching sun in the paddy fields. They felt strongly the effect of the wartime emergencies approaching. One Nisei mentioned that she was looking forward to welcoming back the soldiers who fought for them and who enabled her to make the trip to Japan. And she continued to say, "It is their spirit that is holding me back here to study the customs and habits of my people."[6] She also observed that the Japanese carried on with their various tasks as though there were no war in progress. In the streets of Ginza, she saw show houses, dining places, and concert halls packed with people seeking pleasure to ease their minds from the war against China

The itinerary also took them to various places in Korea, Manchukuo, and China, where they saw totally different scenery and received contrasting impressions. They visited the historic mausoleum of the Manshu Dynasty, palaces of the Ming Dynasty, and the Lama Temple. The group also passed through Port Arthur, the battleground of the Russo-Japanese War, other battlefields, and the war museum. They were impressed with Hsinking, site of the Manchurian Incident, emerging as "a growing metropolis of the Far East." The members of the tour did not cast any doubt as to how these locations were seized by the Japanese army. Of course, it is possible that critical comments on Japanese policy in the colonies were prohibited in their essays.

In the commemorative book on the tour, it is stated that the purpose of the tour was "sightseeing and observing of the well-known cities and historic places of Japan, Manchukuo and North China so that the members of the party may be able to understand the Japanese cultural civilization and various industries as well as the truth of the present conflict in the Far East."[7] Looking back upon the trip, the head of the tour, while expressing his appreciation to all those who made the trip possible, regretted the limited Japanese linguistic abilities of the participants. To begin with, very few of them were able to understand the itinerary of the tour in Japanese. He was disappointed to find that no one on the tour touched anything other than English books and newspapers, and they spoke only English during the course of the trip.

Upon their arrival in Japan, they spoke loudly in English even on trains. Japanese passengers in the same train often frowned at them for their conversation in a foreign tongue. There were even times when they were questioned by police. The school principal was convinced that the curriculum of Japanese-language schools should be drastically reformed in such a way that students could learn practical Japanese. The school principal also came across several cases of discrimination by the Japanese against the Nisei. He felt that while those with high social status tended to be sympathetic with the Nisei situation, ordinary Japanese, including low-ranking government officials, were in general inhospitable. Such cold receptions, the head of the tour worried, might well have provoked antipathy to Japan rather than the sympathy they were trying to build. While disappointed with the low motivation and poor language skills of the participants, he felt sympathy toward the Nisei students who had to face discriminatory treatment both in Japan and the United States.[8]

The Nisei Survey

One of the educational institutions in Tokyo which accepted Nisei in the 1930s was Keisen Girls' School. What is significant about the school is that the graduating Nisei students there left important historical data on the Nisei in Japan at that time. A collective graduation project was compiled by a group of students in 1939. The project, *The Nisei: A Survey of Their Educational, Vocational, and Social Problems* covered only the Nisei who resided in the Tokyo-Yokohama area, and yet perhaps it is the most detailed survey of the adolescent Nisei living in Tokyo and its vicinity in the prewar period. According to the survey, there were approximately 1,500 Nisei living in the Tokyo and Yokohama area alone. Although it was difficult to locate all of the Nisei living in this area, the survey committee mailed 1,141 questionnaires to Nisei in the region, of which 437 were returned. The questionnaire covered four basic areas: (1) general questions (sex, status, birthplace, hometown, occupations of parents, purpose in coming to Japan, and date of arrival in Japan); (2) education (previous education, purpose and method of study—curriculum, extra-curricula activities, finances); (3) social life (general adjustment, activities—recreation, amusements, religion, marriage, citizenship, future plans); and (4) vocation (type of vocation, difficulties in securing positions, special advantages of being a Nisei, and the type of work open to Nisei in Japan).

Of the 437 surveys sent back, 205 were from males and 232 were from females. They were mainly from California and Hawaii, with 151 from the former and 112 from the latter. Other areas represented included Washington state (54), Japan (20), Canada (15), Oregon (14), Utah (14), and the Philippines and Singapore. The survey shows that the dates of arrival in Japan concentrated on six years between 1933 and 1938. Although the earliest arrival was in 1922, there were many Nisei who came to Japan before 1922 and were not included in the survey. What strikes us here is the sharp increase beginning in 1933. Why did that happen? In order to answer the question, we need to look at some possible societal factors as causes.

Possible Reasons for Increased Numbers of Nisei Studying in Japan
Be it the difficulty of finding employment, a marriage partner, or proper education, so-called "Nisei problems" were on the tongues of every Issei in the Japanese community. Educational problems, however, received more attention than any other concerns. It is too simplistic to say that the increase of the Nisei population in the United States alone brought about the trend of sending them to Japan for study. There were surely other factors involved—in other words, some benefits or rewards for the Issei who took the trouble to send Nisei to Japan.

Before making up their minds to do so, Issei parents had to ask themselves several questions. "What is good about sending my kids to Japan? Will my son become a little more sympathetic to us? Will my daughter come to behave gracefully like a Japanese woman?" A Nisei might ask, "What is it like to live in a country where everybody is Japanese-looking? What kind of job can I get by going all the way to Japan? Will I able to speak Japanese fluently after a few years there?"

From the point of community leaders, there must have been some returns for the community itself if so many Nisei youths flocked to the real Tokyo instead of Little Tokyo in downtown Los Angeles. The leaders must have wondered if there were any social rewards which would enforce and recognize membership in the family and community. They may have expected that the Nisei upon their return to the United States would be able to defend the position of Japanese militaristic activities in China. Or perhaps ministers at churches might have had a vague expectation that Nisei students living in church facilities in Japan would become active members of their respective churches upon their return to the States.

The Issei were looking for a way to narrow the linguistic and cultural as well as generational gap between themselves and the Nisei. Sending Nisei children to Japanese schools was of course one possible solution. As we have seen, however, instruction at language schools was inadequate for fulfilling the Issei's expectations. The gaps were too wide for private institutions to fill.

It is conventional wisdom that one of the best ways to master a foreign language is to go to the country where the target language is spoken. Some customs and social rules can only be learned in the target culture. The notions of filial piety, respect for the elderly, self-sacrifice, among other Confucianistic teachings inherent in the Japanese culture, were considered to be something that could not be easily learned in the American school system. Issei also thought that if Nisei became acquainted with these virtues in Japanese culture along with the Japanese language, they would also have some positive influence upon other Nisei who remained in the United States. Issei hoped that not only on the individual and family levels but also at the community level Niseis studying in Japan would bring some positive impact on the Japanese community in general.

While these cultural aspects constituted important factors for sending Nisei to Japan, fiscal benefits seemed to play a more practical part in the decision-making process. To understand how the fiscal benefits were created, we should briefly examine the economic situation in Japan and the United States in the 1920s and 1930s.

Both Japan and the United States enjoyed an unprecedented economic boom during World War I because of military expenditures. However, Japan was not able to enjoy economic growth for long. In 1919, the year after the end of the war, the balance of international payments had already turned to a deficit. To make matters worse, a major earthquake hit Tokyo and the vicinity on September 1, 1923. The yen dropped to 38 dollars against 100 yen. The yen recovered to about 45 dollars for a while. However, the Showa Depression, ignited by a careless remark by the Financial Minister in 1927, and the Great Depression, which broke out in New York in 1929, put the Japanese economy into a downward spiral. In addition, in December 1931 the Japanese government left the gold standard. All of these factors contributed to the depreciation of the yen to as little as 20 yen against the dollar.

This declining value of the yen was a nightmare for Japanese abroad who were receiving remittances from Japan and for those Issei who were saving money at Japanese banks. However, the appreciation of the dollar made traveling to Japan much easier for the majority of Issei and Nisei. Under these circumstances, it was sufficiently advantageous to send Nisei youths to Japan for study, especially when they realized that the total cost for higher education in Japan was less than half of that at home.

For Nisei themselves, their educational choice was closely connected with their future occupational possibilities. An increasing number of Nisei were at the stage where they needed to contemplate their not-so-far-away future occupations. In contrast with the early 1920s when the large majority of Nisei were still young, many of them were now in high schools and colleges. If their experience in Japan would help their job prospects, it was certainly worthwhile to consider going to Japan for a few years. For some Nisei, Japan was about their last resort for employment. In fact, many college graduates ended up working in fruit markets and florist shops owned by their own parents.

Of those Nisei surveyed in Tokyo and Yokohama in the aforementioned survey carried out by Keisen Girls' School in 1939, 80 percent were students and 20 percent were employed. To be more exact, 99 of 437 were working at the time the survey was conducted, and 28 of them had experience working in the United States. Some of those who went to Japan to work did so with indefinite plans. As a result, they were not able to find the kind of job or position they would like to have had due to their lack of training and language problems.

Even if Nisei were employed, there often occurred cultural frictions between them and employers. As one Nisei put it, "The Japanese employer resents the individualistic, wanting-to-learn-everything attitude of the Nisei. The Nisei, if offered a better salary from another firm, will pack up and leave, whereas the Japanese employee is expected to do nothing but what he is specifically told to do."[9] Other problems arose from poor health and even lack of "King's English." The survey committee admitted that there was a tendency for Nisei to become less fluent in English the longer they stayed in Japan. Therefore, they thought that some Nisei who were teaching or tutoring English were not really qualified. How much truth there was in this appraisal remains unclear. However, what interests us is that among the Japanese there was an expectation that American-born Nisei should speak "the King's English."

On the whole, securing employment in Japan was not as easy as Nisei had expected. As was true for the average Japanese college graduate, finding employment in larger companies was no easy task for Nisei. Since no special privileges were given to them, they had to compete with others on an equal basis, which was in actuality a losing battle for many. Thus, the majority of Nisei tried to seek employment in foreign firms where salaries were in fact higher than prestigious large Japanese companies. And yet, the average Nisei male received a salary of about 70 to 90 yen a month, which was much less than the average salary of approximately 100 to 150 for Nisei females who found clerical jobs. The reason for this discrepancy, according to the survey, lay in the fact that the Nisei female monopolized the field of clerical work then. Nisei males on the other hand were forced to compete with the Japan-born men on equal terms.

Because of this male-female difference in job demand, Nisei men tended to perceive that occupations open to Nisei men were far fewer than those for women. Many Nisei women were actually optimistic about securing employment in Japan. Some commented, "All fields are open, depending on the qualifications." Another said, "Almost any field is open to Nisei with even a speaking knowledge of Japanese; however, these positions are not always available immediately."[10]

One might assume that these survey results would lead Nisei males to answer negatively to the question as to whether they would stay in Japan for future occupations. On the contrary, 49 of the men responded that they would rather work in Japan, as opposed to 36 men who answered otherwise. As for the women, 48 preferred to work in Japan and 49 of them expressed their preference of working in the country where they were educated. Although we should judge the results with caution, the following comment by a Nisei male explains why he preferred working in Japan rather than in the States. "I would rather work in Japan because there is no racial prejudice; it is a country where man is man and where one has an equal chance of advancement; it is a country of cosmopolitan food." Another commented that he would prefer working in Japan because he believed that he would be able to find himself more deep-rooted in Japan as he had a feeling that he would be able to adapt himself to the society.[11]

Another possible argument for why Nisei males preferred to stay in Japan can be found in their preference of marriage partners. Many Nisei males said that they would like to find their life companions among those females who were either born and raised in Japan or born in the United States but educated in Japan. Nisei men tended to feel that the Nisei girls who were raised in the States were too bossy and too idealistic in their conception of an ideal husband. The survey showed that 58 preferred Nisei, 58 Japan-born, and 38 Japan-educated Nisei. Nisei women, on the other hand, overwhelmingly chose Nisei males as marriage partners, with 106 for Nisei, 46 Japan-born, and 41 Japan-educated Nisei. And if Nisei men decided to get married to a Japanese national, they were bound to stay in Japan, the reason being that the immigration law in the States prohibited the free entrance of the Japanese after 1924. In fact, to the question of which country they preferred for their future home, 75 men answered that they wanted to stay in Japan as opposed to 53 in the United States. As for Nisei females, 78 of them preferred the United States while 65 preferred Japan as their future home.

Educational Institutions

Let us now return to the education of Nisei in Japan. A typical Nisei male student in Japan was a high school graduate and upon his arrival in Japan received preparatory language instruction for half a year and proceeded to a college or university. His 12 years of education in the United States was approximately equal to the eleven years of education to middle school level (six years in elementary school and five years in middle school) in Japan at that time.

Therefore, the Ministry of Education considered that high school graduates from the United States had sufficient qualifications for applying to colleges and universities. A typical Nisei female student, on the other hand, was a junior high school graduate, and in Japan she tended to enter a girls' high school or a vocational school.

The Nisei Survey results showed that over 76 percent were enrolled in some school in Tokyo or Yokohama and 4 percent were studying under private tutors. The institutions that accepted Nisei were the following: 14 universities, 6 women's colleges, 16 boys' middle schools, and 37 girls' high schools.[12] Yamashita's figures show that approximately 40 percent of the male Nisei majored in commerce and economics, 20 percent in law, and 30 percent in humanities, engineering, medicine combined. About 30 percent of Nisei females were studying English literature, 20 percent home economics, 10 percent Japanese literature, and the rest included dressmaking, handicrafts, nursing, dentistry, music, pharmacology, and dancing.[13]

There were also some private institutions for helping Nisei youths enter high schools and colleges, such as The Nichibei Home, The Nichigo Bunka Gakko, and The Waseda International Institute. The majority of these privately founded preparatory institutions were established by religious organizations.

The Nichibei Home, for example, was founded in Tokyo by the Buddhist Association of America in 1932 specifically for Nisei students coming from Hawaii. Living in a dormitory under rather strict rules and regulations (the hours were set for rising at 6:40 A.M., breakfast at 7:00 A.M., lunch at 11:00 A.M., dinner at 7:00 P.M., and putting out lights at 10:00 P.M.), the Nisei students prepared mainly for college entrance examinations at such private universities as Waseda University, Nihon University, Meiji University, Toyo University, and Rikkyo University. Although the Nichibei Home was a Buddhist-based school, none of the universities above was related to Buddhist sects.

A somewhat unique institution was the Mizuho Gakuen. It was established by a government-founded organization called The Kaigai Kyoiku Kyokai (The Institute for the Education of Overseas Japanese). The institute was the only public educational facility for Nisei in Japan which received annual subsidies from the government. The Mizuho Gakuen consisted of the Hodo Gakubu (a supplementary school for the study of Japanese), dormitories, and a library.

The Mizuho Gakuen was situated at the top of Mount Masugata, Ikuta Village, Tachibana County, Kanagawa Prefecture, 20 minutes away from the central Tokyo. The school, library, and dormitories were on a 600,000 square-foot plot. It was created "in view of the fact that many Japanese living abroad are greatly troubled by the question of educating their children, or the so-called second-generation Japanese."[14] The founders of the institution felt that "Japan's future foreign expansion would be absolutely impossible as long as this educational problem remained unsettled."[15] Thus, as a publicly funded institution, their objectives were not only to solve the so-called second-generation problem but also to alleviate the educational problems for the sake of the foreign expansion of the Japanese people. Although not its main purpose, the institute also handled the affairs of education and protection of foreigners residing in Japan for study. The President at the time was Viscount Kikujiro Ishii, member of the Privy Council, and the Managing Director was Ryusaku Endo, member of the House of Peers. A government subsidy of 50,000 yen was given to the institute during the fiscal years 1934 and 1935.

With the help of generous donations, first three dormitories were built, followed by two other dormitories, the library, and laboratory facilities. Each of the five dormitories was fully equipped with Western-style bedrooms, living and study rooms, dining rooms, community rooms, a kitchen, Western/Japanese-style toilets, wash-rooms, bathrooms, and a storeroom. A director resided in each dormitory, which was self-governed by the students. The number of students as of October 1940 was 84 in total: 37 from the mainland United States, 27 from California, 19 from Hawaii, 13 from Canada, 5 from Brazil, 4 from Mexico, 2 each from Philippines and Guam, and 1 each from Singapore and Java. Of the 84 students, 73 of them lived in the dormitories and 11 were commuting students.[16]

The school term based on the Japanese academic calendar started on April 1 and ended on March 31. The admission fee was 5 yen and the annual tuition was 85 yen. The students were also expected to pay the monthly dormitory fees of 28 yen, which included expenses for food, living, and other items. The course of study was three years, but the period could be shortened if the student passed all the requirements. The applicants were admitted on their educational records and the entrance examination of the Japanese language. Subjects taught at the institute were the following: Civics, An Outline of the Condition of Japan, Japanese (reading, grammar, composition, and penmanship), Chinese Classics, Mathematics, Geography, History, English (English-Japanese/Japanese-English translation), Physical Training, *Budo* (Japanese fencing), and *Jujutsu* (martial arts).[17]

Language Abilities and Attitudes of the Nisei

Since it is impossible to return to the past and test how effective language instruction at Japanese-language schools was, we have to rely on secondary sources which studied the Japanese language abilities of the pupils/students in Japanese-language school. There are several prewar studies on Japanese language schools in Los Angeles and in California in general.

Edward Strong conducted a survey of Japanese in California in which he asked questions about linguistic abilities of Issei and Nisei in English and Japanese. He also touched upon the attendance of Nisei children at Japanese-language schools. In general, he concluded that many of the Nisei felt that attendance at public schools was sufficient and that it was not necessary to attend Japanese-language school. Many older Nisei shared the Issei view, namely, that maintenance of the Japanese language was necessary. A closer look at the attendance of Nisei revealed only 15 percent of male and 27 percent of female Japan-born Nisei attended language school, with the average being less than a year, whereas approximately 69 percent of the United States–born of both sexes attended, with an average of three years.

This study showed the Japanese-speaking ability of the subjects to be as follows. Two of the Japanese interviewers of the study established five degrees of ability to speak Japanese: (1) well-educated Japanese in Japan; (2) the best heard in the United States; (3) average; (4) low average; and (5) little knowledge of the language. The result showed that between the ages of 14 and 34 years of age, the males and females born in Japan were rated 1.24 and 1.36 respectively, while their counterparts born in the United States were 2.28 and 2.16. Ratings were also obtained from 27 Nisei students from the ages of 14 to 19 years who attended "one of the best Japanese-language schools." The average ratings for three different language skills of this group were 2.5 for reading, 2.3 for writing, and 2.5 for speaking. The researcher suggested that the difficulty of the Japanese language contributed to the relatively low scores of the students. Although it is extremely difficult to measure exact linguistic abilities of the general Nisei population, the study revealed the overall language abilities of the Nisei.[18]

Robert H. Ross examined social distance between the first and second generations in Los Angeles. The results of the study are useful for understanding linguistic communication between the Issei and Nisei in the prewar period, although the number of subjects in the study, particularly of the Issei, was limited (41 male and 17 female Issei and 78 male and 72 female Nisei). When Nisei were asked if they would use Japanese when speaking to their parents, 52 males and 55 females, or more than 70 percent, answered that they "almost always" did. The Issei, when asked the same question, replied that 74 percent of them would "almost always" use Japanese with their children. In terms of the communication between Nisei children, namely, between brothers and sisters, 56 percent said that they would "almost always" use English. To the question "Do you read Japanese newspapers?", 45 percent of the Nisei subjects responded that they "very rarely" did, while only 10 percent said they "almost always" did. Concerning listening to speeches in the Japanese language, however, 23 percent responded "very rarely," 15 percent "rarely," and 30 percent "sometimes."[19]

Despite the general belief that Nisei children were forced to attend language schools, many of the Nisei subjects responded that their parents "very rarely" had to urge them to go to Japanese school (45 percent), while very few "almost always" had to do so (12 percent). Furthermore, 42 percent of them felt that language school drew them closer to their parents. In addition, contrary to the general belief, 43 percent of the Issei parents "very rarely" urged their children to go the Japanese school, while 29 percent "almost always" did so. Issei parents also appeared to believe that language school drew their children closer to them (67 percent answered either "often" or "almost always").

Ross stated that "the inability of the older group to convey to their offspring their inner thoughts is responsible in a large measure for the existence of social farness."[20] He quoted a young Nisei who said that although Issei possessed a Japanese "philosophy," they had difficulties in explaining it to their children because of the language difficulty and their lack of education while in Japan. The following observations are also noteworthy. Among children, the oldest child was usually closer to his parents because of his linguistic skills in Japanese and his limited skills in English. Conversely, the younger children were not as close to their parents for the opposite reasons. Ross also noticed that problems arising from linguistic miscommunication between the parents and children were more serious in urban areas than rural areas. Those in rural areas were generally engaged in farming as a family, which made them closer to each other. Being isolated from the English-speaking society, Nisei children in the farming business developed Japanese linguistic skills better than those Nisei living in urban areas.[21]

There are many impressionistic accounts in historical documents. Many of them point out that despite the popularity of Japanese-language schools, few students acquired the language skills to the degree that they could fluently converse with native Japanese. *Nichi Bei Shimbun*, for example, reported in 1936 that when the Nisei students who finished junior-high school level (from eighth grade to tenth grade) at the Japanese-language school went to Japan for study, many of them were studying textbooks at the fifth- or sixth-grade level in Japan.[22]

The Nisei students themselves questioned the effectiveness of the language teaching at the Japanese-language school. A representative student is quoted in the *Nichi Bei Shimbun* as saying:

To me the time expended in the Japanese-language school at an early age is time and effort wasted, as it is so easily forgotten for lack of use and practical need. If one finds it absolutely necessary to learn the Japanese language after graduation there is time enough, when one can devote all his effort and concentrated thought. It can then be mastered in half the time. When the second generation continues his Japanese education with his American education it usually interferes with his English studies.[23]

When Captain Kai Rasmussen tested the linguistic abilities of nearly 4,000 Nisei in uniform, he found that fewer than 10 percent of them could read, write, or speak more than a few words of their ancestral language. Not more than 100 could be considered to be "somewhat competent" in Japanese.[24] Of course, we should take into consideration that although the majority of the Nisei attended Japanese language schools, only a few of them proceeded to the junior-high and senior-high school levels. By the time they were drafted, their Japanese skills could have suffered from disuse. Furthermore, those Nisei who volunteered might well have been Americanized types.

In general, Yamato Ichihashi was convinced "these schools have been unsuccessful in their primary function—that of imparting a knowledge of the Japanese language to American-born children of Japanese descent."[25] He pointed out, however, that "they have done remarkably well in some other respects, in particular in teaching proper conduct and behavior." The sociologist Harry Kitano also acknowledges this point by quoting from an interview, "Even if I did go to school just to meet my friends and fool around, my parents never minded it just as long as they knew I was going to Japanese school."[26] In addition to the value of making friends at the school, he also mentions another value of the school: its baby-sitting function. Japanese-language schools kept the children off the streets, which may have been one of the reasons for the low rate of crime and delinquency among the Nisei children in the prewar period.

There were several reasons why in general the Nisei in the United States did not acquire as much in the way of Japanese-language skills as the Issei hoped. First, the Japanese language is not an easy language to learn for foreigners. Naoya Shiga, a noted author in Japan, once blamed the language for causing the war and even suggested that French be adopted as Japan's national language. Although such a suggestion was never taken seriously by the majority of the Japanese people, they agreed that the language is so different from other languages that very few foreigners could master it. This is certainly an exaggeration and even humiliating for people who speak other languages. It is true, however, that it takes a long time for English speakers to be acquainted with the written system and *keigo* (honorific forms) of the language. The Nisei as a native English speaker had to learn three different writing systems—*hiragana, katakana,* and *kanji* (characters)—the last of which amounted to 1,360 in an elementary school textbook. Thus, in contrast to English which consists of an alphabet of only 26 letters, the pupils had to spend extensive time just in learning *kanji.* Adding to the difficulty are the various forms of pronouns, male-female distinctions, and distinctive differences between the written form and colloquial form of the language, among many other characteristics.

The lack of instructional hours was a chronic problem. One hour to an hour and a half was the maximum that the Nisei could spend after public school in learning Japanese at a Japanese-language school. Parents might choose to have the child skip Japanese classes on cold, dark, and rainy evenings. A teacher might want to give supplementary lessons to less advanced pupils after class, but he or she would have second thoughts when considering the homework the children had to do in public school and at home.

The strained economic circumstances of many of the Japanese-language schools caused the hiring of less qualified teachers and use of poor facilities. Some teachers did not take the job seriously since the pay was low and the job was only one to two hours a day. The financial difficulty also meant that the schools held only one class for 30 to 40 pupils in all grade levels from the first to the eighth. The ever fluctuating attitude of the Japanese community toward the children's Japanese education, varying from the desire to abolish the language school to establishing an ultra-nationalistic school, might well have affected the pupils negatively. These and other insurmountable problems surrounding the Japanese-language schools did not make the Issei optimistic about the Nisei's learning of the language. Precisely because of these adversities, there were great rewards for the Nisei who overcame the difficulties, but for the majority of the Nisei, the obstacles were too high to obtain such rewards.

Nisei Life in Japan

Having looked at the Nisei's linguistic, cultural, and educational background in the United States, let us look at how Nisei felt about everyday life in Japan. Nisei, although they looked the same as the rest of the Japanese youngsters, were obviously different in their behavior and ways of thinking. Women especially seemed to feel difficulty in adjusting themselves to the new mode of living. Take sitting on *tatami* flooring for a long time, for instance. Getting themselves used to doing this without finding themselves numb in their lower limbs required a certain amount of training and perseverance. Distinctive differences between male and female speech in the Japanese language was another major difficulty. Women in particular were expected to be careful of their speech, with the proper use of honorifics.

How did Issei and the Japanese public view Nisei in Japan? Takizo Matsumoto, a professor of Meiji University and a native of Fresno, California, gave lectures to the Issei parents upon his return to his native hometown. He emphatically stated that the Issei parents should not send their children to Japan without a definite purpose in mind. He warned that about 80 percent of those Nisei in Tokyo not only failed to master the Japanese language and culture but also became stray sheep wandering around the streets of Ginza. While praising a few of the Nisei students studying hard to acquire the language and culture with a definite purpose for the future, he was disappointed with the majority. For example:

Today, when the people in Japan [see] a young man in a stylish suit wearing a hat on the back of his head walking along with a waitress of a cafe on the streets of Ginza, they cast ridicule, scorn, upon him, saying "You Nisei!" And they do so even if he is not a Nisei. How sad it has to happen to Nisei. But it is true.[27]

The Japanese people had a certain stereotypical image of Nisei. The stereotype was of a young man chewing gum on the street, speaking a mixture of Japanese and English loudly, uttering poor Japanese, having no sense of propriety, and pushing his hat back on his head.

In February 1934, a symposium on the problems of Nisei in Japan was held in Tokyo.[28] The speakers included such figures as Kozen Tsunemitsu, the head of Nichibei Home; Soen Yamashita, a correspondent of *Nippu Jiji* in Tokyo; Junin Ono, a former minister at Los Angeles Honganji Buddhist Temple; and two businessmen. Tsunemitsu pointed out that the Foreign Ministry, and the Ministry of Education, as well as the Tokyo Metropolitan Police, started paying more attention to Nisei as their number increased sharply. Ono brought up an incident regarding a Nisei male student from Los Angeles who committed suicide at a restroom after being seized by the police. That incident reminded Tsunemitsu of another Nisei incident. A Nisei female from Hawaii became a waitress at a cafe and strayed out of contact for a while. She was finally found but returned to Hawaii with her parents. Yamashita also recalled a newspaper article that reported that there were some suspicious Nisei who might be spies from the mainland United States and Hawaii. The espionage incident turned out to be just a groundless rumor. But the Metropolitan Police and other offices began to pay attention to what Nisei did in Japan.

The participants agreed on the point that Nisei were often flattered by the attention that they received for their knowledge and skills in English and Western music. Innocent Nisei were overcome by various temptations in urban life. With a strong dollar, Nisei had enough resources to spend lavishly at cafes and dance halls.

Tsunemitsu concluded that one-third of the Nisei in Japan were working hard without supervision, another third were hopeless, and the rest were indifferent about their own education but could be controlled if properly guided. Overall, Nisei with their background in American pragmatic education did not seem to be able to get along with the cramming system of Japanese education.

The way some of the educators in Japan looked at Nisei students in Japan disappointed Nisei. Miya Kikuchi, in her letter to Robert A. Wilson, Director of the Japanese American Research Project, recalls her days in Japan. She touches on a round table discussion for leaders of organizations connected with the education of young Nisei studying in Japan. Approximately fifteen attended, representing various organizations such as Buddhist groups, private schools, YMCA, YWCA, and Japanese-language schools for foreigners. Without knowing that Kikuchi was a Nisei, almost all the participants rather harshly criticized Nisei students, with such remarks as "outlandish ways of these Nisei," their "horrible, low class, boorish, country-style Japanese speech," and their "single-minded chattering." Kikuchi was particularly embarrassed when all but one (who happened to be Michi Kawai of Keisen Girls' School) solemnly nodded as one speaker said, "The Nisei are children of low class, peasant emigrants, so what could we expect of them?"[29]

How did the Nisei perceive the Japanese situation? One Nisei wrote to his Nisei friend in the United States in 1937, discouraging his fellow Nisei in America from coming to Japan. He asserted that there were too many obstacles for the Nisei to overcome in Japan. Lack of social activities and education made the life of the Nisei less pleasurable in Japan than in his American homeland. He went on to write:

A great disappointment awaits any Nisei who expects to lead the same exciting social whirl he or she had tasted and was used to back home . . . The so-called cafes in Japan are worthless houses in which to spend our time. Though we enjoy dancing, dancing halls are ill reputed pleasure places for the Japanese, and this added with the expensive charges per dance, keeps us away from them. Moving pictures, Japanese theatres and perhaps, the Japanese revues are the only places w[h]ere we can spend our time and satisfy our craving for wholesome entertainment.[30]

The sender of this letter does not seem to be one of the diligent Nisei students intending to become a "bridge of understanding." His honest account of what he saw and felt in Japan may be a representative view of the majority of the Nisei who spent part of their lives in Japan.

Responding to an interview with Soen Yamashita, female students at Musashino Joshi Gakuin Koto Jogakko in the fall of 1933 expressed their own feelings as Nisei students in Japan. One of the shared opinions had to do with the Japanese language. They felt they should have studied Japanese harder while they were in Hawaii or the mainland United States. For instance, they had difficulties in distinguishing different ways of calling numbers in Japanese such as *shi* and *yon* for four, *shichi* and *nana* for seven. They also had trouble understanding Japan-made English words and the way English is pronounced and represented in katakana orthography. *Rajio* for radio, *sutoppu* for stop, and *airon* for a pressing iron did not ring a bell for them at all.

A teacher in charge of Nisei at Musashino commented that it was generally true that those from the mainland United States proved to be better and quicker learners of the Japanese language than those from Hawaii. One of the students conjectured that it was because of the mixture of different languages used in Hawaii. Another student complained about the Japanese people's attitudes toward the Nisei's spoken Japanese. Whenever the Japanese flattered her saying how good her Japanese was, she felt as if she were being insulted. That is to say, "flattering" for her was another way of saying that Nisei would never be able to master the language.

Yamashita had a chance to interview some Nisei in Kyoto, too. One female Nisei was candid about how disappointed she was during her first years in Japan. Another felt like going home on the second day in Japan. Still another was not able to understand the Kyoto dialect and was frustrated in his attempts to communicate with the local residents. He also felt that the Japanese students were childish in their behavior when compared to their American counterparts.

Issei leaders who saw the situation of Nisei in Japan were generally sympathetic toward them. They figured that most of the misunderstanding was derived from differences in customs and lack of the linguistic abilities to make themselves understood to the Japanese. These readers assumed a critical stance toward the Issei parents who sent their children to Japan aimlessly. Yamashita categorized three types of Issei parents who sent Nisei to Japan: those who had a definite purpose in mind, those who wanted Nisei to see at first hand what Japan was like, and those who sent Nisei without any aim or plan. And he had a feeling that the third group outnumbered the other two groups combined.[31]

The 1930s is considered to be a decade of rampant nationalism in Japan. And yet, with certain exceptions, in the historical documents and data available to this author at present, Nisei who studied in Japan did not seem to be as much affected as Japanese youths were. They were busy adjusting themselves to the new environment and many of them were studying or trying to find a decent job.

In October 1940, the U.S. Senate passed a bill (HR9980) which established that those U.S. citizens who were born to parents who were ineligible to citizenship would lose their own citizenship if they stayed in their parental land for more than six months. The law did not immediately affect those Nisei who had stayed in Japan for more than half a year and thus they did not automatically lose their U.S. citizenship. However, they had to return to the United States within six months following January 13, 1941. Although exact figures are not available for how many Nisei residing in Japan subsequently returned to the United States by June 1941, it is safe to assume that the majority of the Nisei left Japan and hurried home before the war broke out.

Chapter Six
Possibilities and Limitations
Japanese-Language Schools in Other Parts of the World

I entered a barbershop. The barbers were women, and after I got into the chair I was sorry I had gone in. The woman talked to me in Japanese; she knew no English. I indicated with pantomime that I wanted my hair cut only in back and around the sides. She nodded, then talked to her fellow barber, no doubt about me: how strange it was that I did not understand Japanese. I tried not to listen; did not like the sound of the language. . . . Touching a residue of understanding in me, their words made me miserable.
—Louis Adams, *A Young American with a Japanese Face* (1939)

In the preceding chapters, we have looked in detail at language- and heritage-maintenance efforts of Japanese immigrants in California. In this chapter, I would like to turn attention to other parts of the world where a large number of Japanese emigrated—Hawaii and Brazil.

Hawaii was the first foreign land to which large numbers of Japanese people emmigrated in modern times. Accordingly, it is also the place where education, particularly that of the Japanese language, was raised as an important issue among the immigrant group. Japanese-language schools in Hawaii, because of its proximity to Japan, provided second-generation children with more substantial linguistic and cultural education than any other immigrant country.

Brazil, on the other hand, is located much further away. In the early twentieth century, when neither mass air transportation nor satellite communication systems existed, people needed to be much more committed to staying in a new land for a long period. The distance made the immigrants nostalgic for their own homeland. Eagerness to maintain their own mother-tongue was strong. Naturally, Japanese-language schools sprang up in almost every colony where children were found.

The differing political, economic, and cultural circumstances in which these two groups of Japanese immigrants settled created two different sets of language and cultural institutions. Yet, for the most part, the two types of language schools shared common characteristics. This chapter will examine some of the shared and unshared experiences in the language and ethnic education of Nisei in the two different settings.

Japanese-Language Schools in Hawaii, 1892–1941

In 1868, the first year of the new Japanese Meiji era, Eugene Van Reed, an American merchant who worked at the Hawaiian consulate in Japan, took 141 men and 6 women known as *Gannen-mono* (first-year people) to Hawaii without the permission of the new Meiji government.[1] These laborers recruited in Tokyo and Yokohama worked on sugar cane plantations in Hawaii, but because of their apparent dissatisfaction with working conditions and wages, many returned to Japan. The first Japanese government-sponsored immigrants reached the Islands in 1885 after incessant requests from the Hawaiians. They included 689 men, 156 women, and 108 children. During the three years between 1885 and 1888, the Imperial Statistical Annals of Japan show that 8,012 Japanese laborers went to Hawaii and 690 returned to Japan.[2]

What is relevant here is the fact that there were not only men but also women and children in the *Kan'yaku Imin* (government-sponsored immigrants). As mentioned in Chapter 2, in 1921 the Japanese government prohibited so-called "picture brides," but until that time immigrant men continued to arrange for wives to be sent from Japan. By 1900, the Japanese population in Hawaii was 47,508 men and 13,603 women, but by 1920, there were 62,644 men and 46,630 women. In 1920, the Japanese composed 40.8 percent of the total population of the Islands, and the Japanese immigrant population consisted of 33 percent adult males, 20 percent adult females, and 46 percent minors.[3]

In the earlier immigrant period, the unbalanced ratio between males and females created various problems and education of children was not a top priority. Consequently, many children grew up without receiving much attention from parents at home, let alone Japanese-language education. As the number of Nisei increased, education, particularly that of language, became a significant issue. The first Japanese-language school was created in Kula, Maui, in 1892 and was followed by a school in Halawa, Kohala, Hawaii, the next year.[4] In 1896, Nihonjin Shogakko was established by the Christian minister Rev. Takie Okumura with an enrollment of thirty pupils. Textbooks and instructional materials were donated by the Japanese Mombusho at Okumura's request. The school used Mombusho textbooks, taught reading, calligraphy, composition, moral education, and physical education for two hours beginning at three P.M. on weekdays. Japanese national holidays were faithfully observed.[5] What motivated Okumura to establish the Japanese-language school was his disappointment with the children's behavior and their use of mixed languages, all of which he believed derived from a lack of education on the part of their parents. In this early period in the history of Japanese-language schools, plantation owners welcomed the establishment of the school by offering land and even by paying construction costs. Doing so pleased Japanese laborers and contributed to increased production.[6]

As the number of Japanese-language schools increased, three different groups of schools emerged—Christian, Buddhist, and nonsectarian—with the first two groups being constantly at odds. School conflicts were so extensive among the Japanese in Hawaii that over fifty incidents related to the language schools were reported around 1914.[7] In addition to these conflicts, pressure from outside arose generally in the form of accusations that the schools were teaching children allegiance to Japan. Separation of the schools from religious influence was called for from both within and without the Japanese community. Circumstances surrounding the schools became increasingly unfavorable during this time. Of six school teachers dispatched from Japan in July 1917, only one was allowed to land because she was born in Hawaii; the other five teachers were rejected despite pleas to the U.S. Secretary of Labor. The sponsoring school and the teachers appealed to the Ninth Circuit Court of the United States in San Francisco, which ruled that the teachers could land because they were not immigrants. The Immigration Office appealed to the Supreme Court, which in turn confirmed the judgment of the circuit court. Although the Japanese-language schools won this case, the incident was a clear forewarning of the pressure to Americanize that was to come. In 1919, Henry W. Kinney, Superintendent of Public Instruction of the Territory of Hawaii, requested that the Educational Department of the Honpa Honganji Buddhist Mission submit textbooks currently used in Japanese-language schools for review.

The Governor and the Superintendent of the Department of Public Instruction requested that the United States Department of the Interior's Bureau of Education investigate the language schools. A four-member Federal Survey Commission, sent by the Bureau, recommended in 1919 that the schools be controlled by the Board of Education and gradually eliminated. Moreover, the Commission suggested that school buildings used by those Japanese-language schools be turned over to the board for future use in public school activities.[8] Following these recommendations were several bills aimed at abolishing Japanese-language schools in Hawaii. The Territorial Attorney General, Harry Irwin, proposed this in November 1920. In view of the adverse circumstances, the Japanese Educational Association held a meeting and decided to submit a compromise proposal to the Honolulu Chamber of Commerce. The proposal was accepted and introduced to the House of Representatives where it was unanimously passed. The bill (Act 30) was signed by the Governor and became effective in July of the next year. This compromise forced schools to obtain a permit to operate and teachers to acquire English skills and knowledge of American history and institutions. It also restricted hours of instruction to one hour a day during afternoons or six hours in any one week.[9]

In November 1922, the so-called Clark bill, which proposed the gradual elimination of the lower grades and payment of one dollar per pupil a year to the state, was passed and added to Act 30. This amended bill was proposed by American members of the Japanese textbook editing committee. Japanese community members were furious that the Japanese appointees on the committee did not oppose the bill; the Japanese committee members all eventually resigned because of the incident. Several Japanese-language schools then went to court to challenge the constitutionality of Act 30. As a result, a majority of the language schools joined the legal action.

Meanwhile, in Nebraska in 1923 the Supreme Court of the United States reversed a decision by the state of Nebraska that prohibited the teaching of any foreign language to children who had not yet passed the eighth grade (See Chapter 4 for more details). This Supreme Court ruling worked favorably for the Japanese-language schools in Hawaii. On February 21, 1927, the U.S. Supreme Court finally ruled that Act 30 was unconstitutional.[10]

For the five years between the initiation of litigation in February 1922 and the Supreme Court ruling in February 1927, the Japanese community was divided into two factions, which called each other "radicals." Major local Japanese-language newspapers fell behind each of the two factions—*Nippu Jiji* supported the pro-Act 30 group and *Hawaii Hochi* supported the anti-Act 30 group. While the former was backed by the Japanese Consul General and Christian clergy, the latter was assisted by Buddhist clergy and the Buddhist Japanese-language schools.[11] John N. Hawkins, in his discussion of this language school controversy, states that "political mobilization of the oppressed group and weakening of social control on the part of the dominant elite" were eventually reasons for the success of the Japanese-language schools in Hawaii.[12] Indeed, the large population of Japanese in the Territory allowed their voice to be heard, while the more severe minority status of Japanese immigrants in California discouraged them from attempting a test case.

Japanese-Language Schools in Brazil, 1908–1988

Brazil accepted a large number of Japanese immigrants in the prewar as well as postwar periods. Japanese immigration to Brazil started in 1908 with the so-called 781 *Kasato-maru* immigrants, named after the ship which transported them to Brazil. They were *colono* (plantation laborers) on coffee plantations in the São Paulo area and were expected to fill in the gap caused by the termination of Italian emigration.[13]

As the immigrants started settling in the colonies, they needed to create their own schools and hire Brazilian teachers but were often unable to find full-time teachers. In the case of one female teacher who commuted to the colony from town, the distance contributed to frequent absenteeism. An immigrant with relatively more education usually replaced the absent Brazilian teacher.

The school building had to be built by the immigrants. Working Sundays and holidays, the men in the plantation community assembled to build a one-room school house with whatever inexpensive materials were available. The completed school building usually also served as an assembly hall for the colony, with both Brazilian and Japanese flags displayed in front. When a Brazilian teacher came to teach at the school, she used morning hours for Portuguese lessons, with afternoon hours given to Japanese lessons taught by a Japanese teacher. The Japanese immigrant adults in the colony felt very good about children saying "ohayo gozaimasu" (good morning) in Japanese to them when meeting on the street. Children who went to Brazilian public school in town tended to be looked down upon by the settlers because of their Brazilian salutation and behavior.[14]

The 1924 Immigration Act in the United States, which prohibited Japanese from entering the country, was an incentive for the Japanese government to encourage immigration to Brazil. The economic slump in the post-World War I period and the Great Depression of 1929 prompted the government to find an outlet for its overflowing labor force. The Japanese government paid all the costs for immigrants' passage to Brazil. Because coffee plantations in Brazil required large numbers of farm hands, annual immigration from Japan exceeded 10,000 in 1928 and, except for 1931, continued to do so until 1934. The incoming Japanese immigrants imported fashions and songs as well as up-to-date Japanese expressions and language to the Japanese colonies. Japanese-language schools and other organizations in the colony were all enlivened by the new Japanese immigrants. With the construction of better buildings and the hiring of Brazilian teachers, schools in the colonies became animated. Among some intellectuals in Rio de Janeiro, however, the large influx of Japanese immigrants generated antagonism toward the Asian immigrants.[15]

In 1934, an immigration act aimed at limiting Japanese immigration passed the legislature. Affected by this law, annual immigration from Japan decreased from 22,960 in 1934 to 5,745 in 1935 and to 1,277 in 1941.[16] As Japan's military aggression in China increased, Brazilian government treatment of the Japanese immigrants became less tolerant. The Brazilians suspected that Japanese immigrants were conducting fifth columnist activities for the purpose of making Brazil another Manchuria in the future. Brazilian Presidential Decree 4166 ordered the freezing of Japanese assets in Brazil.

For fifty days between December 1933 and January 1934, Portuguese-language training for Japanese-language school teachers was sponsored by the PTA of the Japanese-language schools in São Paulo, and all foreign language teachers were required to pass the Portuguese examination. Using second- and third-grade textbooks, thousands of Japanese-language school teachers studied Portuguese as well as the history and geography of Brazil. The majority of the teachers passed the examination. Although the school teachers were now granted certification to teach Japanese, the oppressive atmosphere and financial difficulties surrounding the language schools kept young qualified Japanese from choosing teaching as a profession.[17]

As of 1938 there were 476 Japanese-language schools with a total enrollment of 25,000 in Brazil, a number which exceeded that of the occupied land in China and Manchuria. The number of teachers was 554; thus on average there was one teacher per school. Of the 476 schools, 283 were officially approved. These 283 schools consisted of 89 state schools, 50 county schools, and 144 private schools.[18] One of the reasons behind establishing Japanese *shogakko* (elementary schools) was that those Japanese immigrants who worked in the most rural areas had to establish their own schools, since there might be no schools at all. The rest of the unofficial Japanese-language schools, 193 of them, were created partly out of the dissatisfaction with what was believed to be the mediocre education in Brazil.

The teaching of foreign languages to children under fourteen years of age was prohibited in 1938. Japanese-language schools therefore were abolished in December 1938, although parents conducted Japanese-language education secretly at home or in small groups. Some Japanese immigrants even filed a petition with the Japanese consul, asking for money to leave Brazil to emigrate to North China.[19] In the face of this adversity, the council of Japanese schools held a conference on December 23 and 24 in 1938. Kuzuoka, chief of the council's educational affairs section stated that education for the Japanese Brazilian children should be based on *Wakon Hakusai,* or Japanese spirit and Brazilian learning (the analogy being *Wakon Kansai,* or Japanese spirit and Chinese learning). The meaning behind the motto was that educators should help children be aware of the good characteristics of Japanese origin first and then teach them to utilize them for the betterment of Brazilian society. This idea is also expressed as *Nisshu Hakuju,* or primary emphasis on Japan and secondary on Brazil (*Ni,* Japan; *shu,* primary, *Haku,* Brazil; and *ju,* secondary). The basic tenet of this expression is the same as *Nisshu Beiju* used by Japanese immigrants in the United States. For Kuzuoka, abolition of Japanese-language training was unthinkable, because he felt that the Japanese language was the core of the Japanese spirit and should be fostered in the minds of second-generation children. Because of federal control over Japanese-language schools, Kuzuoka encouraged immigrants to continue Japanese education at home. He advocated *zenson gakko-ka,* "the whole village as a school," as a way of handling the situation. That is, he encouraged the Issei to create an environment in which all villagers would be concerned about the education of the next generation. By utilizing movies, libraries, and slides, he believed, the village could unite for a better cause. Kuzuoka further urged parents to act morally and not to focus too much on earning money, so that they could be good examples for their children.[20]

The law was not concerned with control but with prohibition. The teachers were to lose their jobs immediately. Some educators decided to conduct *junkai jugyo* (itinerant teaching) secretly. However, even educators feared negative repercussions from this secret teaching. Taught inside a shanty or garage, children were directed by the teacher to hide textbooks and pretend to be playing if they sensed someone approaching. One concern was that the illegality of these classes was inconsistent with the fundamentals of education. Secondly, the children were in constant fear lest they be found by federal enforcement officers or lest someone would report them. Thus, such clandestine operations did not become popular among the Japanese immigrants. Nevertheless, resentment among the immigrants grew and seeded a reactionary sentiment which exploded in later years.[21]

Although Japanese-language schools in Brazil experienced hardships in the prewar period, they bounced back after the war and as of 1987 numbered 426 schools. More than half of the schools are located in the state of São Paulo where the majority of the Japanese-Brazilians reside.[22] In the same year, 13 percent of 30,000 incoming freshmen at the University of São Paulo were Japanese-Brazilian students, despite the fact that the group composes only 2.5 percent of the total population of the state.[23]

Although the number of Japanese-language schools is one criterion by which to measure the popularity of Japanese-language and cultural education among younger generations of Japanese Brazilians, it does not indicate problems within these schools. The second symposium on Japanese-language education in Brazil in 1981 reported on the contemporary situation of the Japanese-language school in Brazil. Many problems were reported. For example, Japanese-language schools during the prewar period were operated at relatively low cost thanks to sacrifices on the part of teachers. This low tuition has become accepted as a matter of course for Japanese immigrants and has continued even today. English schools today often charge tuition ten times greater than that of Japanese-language schools. Because of this, immigrant parents often consider the schools insignificant and do not suffer serious direct financial loss even if their children quit in the middle of a term. Another problem which current Japanese-language schools face is the disappearance of active Japanese usage among the Nippo-Brasileiros. The majority of pupils at language schools are third- and fourth-generation children of Japanese immigrants, and they rarely have an opportunity to hear and speak Japanese. The teachers, on the other hand, are becoming older and are sometimes incapable of explaining the use of the Japanese language in Portuguese. In short, Japanese-language education has become the teaching of a foreign language.

The economic strength of Japan in recent years has attracted to these schools many non-Japanese learners in Brazil as well. The obvious economic rewards that might follow from knowledge of Japanese is the reason for this trend. However, the supply of appropriate textbooks for Brazilian learners has not met the demand. Lack of dictionaries is another serious problem for these students. Additionally, Brazilian students sometimes feel as if Japanese people do not believe that the Japanese language can ever be learned by foreigners because of its inherent difficulties.[24]

Living in isolated colonies, early Japanese immigrants felt a strong attachment to their motherland. The teaching of Japanese language and culture to their children was an essential part of their community life. Therefore, the psychological trauma that the immigrant experienced in the face of the abrupt prohibition of language teaching was immeasurable. Clandestine teaching of the language could only provide the children with an image of oppression. Notwithstanding federal control over language schools in the prewar period, Japanese Brazilians recovered their zest for education after the political situation became normalized during the postwar period. They have returned in numbers to levels they had achieved at the peak period in the late 1930s.

However, qualitatively the language schools are in many respects different from those of the prewar period, and the accompanying rewards are different as well. Rather than experiencing the more ideologically based abstract rewards that had been prevalent before the war, more and more concrete benefits based on economic possibilities have begun to motivate participants. The future of the Japanese-language school in Brazil is not necessarily bright. More is required for the improvement of facilities, teaching materials, and, most of all, teachers' salaries. Japanese-language education in Brazil has been influenced not only by the domestic situation in Brazil but also by political and economic circumstances in Japan. Japanese-language schools will continue to be affected by the kinds of rewards generated through the intricate ties with the ancestral home. The sharp increase in the number of Japanese-Brazilian temporary workers in Japan in recent years has in fact affected the operations of some Japanese-language schools in Brazil. This is quite ironic. While the number of second- and third-generation Brazilians who speak fluent Japanese increases, that of teachers in Japanese-language schools in Brazil decreases. What the future holds for the maintenance of language and culture for Japanese-Brazilians is not certain.

While early Japanese immigrants in Brazil had to establish their own schools in largely unpopulated rural areas, their counterparts in Hawaii had public schools to which they could send their children. However, the two groups shared basic common characteristics. First, the early immigrants needed to educate their children because of their prospective return home after a few years of hard work on the plantations. Later, as the Nisei grew older, many immigrants decided to settle, and the number of Japanese-language schools increased at a rapid rate. The schools provided social rewards for the children and transmitted knowledge of the language and cultural tradition—a necessity for achieving recognition as a member of the family and the community.

The schools provided not only for the Nisei's linguistic and cultural education but also for the Issei's social needs. The schools in fact became the center of the community much as the church was the center for European immigrants. Because of their prominence as the nucleus of each immigrant community, however, the schools also became the focal point of the nationalist attack on foreign elements in the nations. The immigrants in Brazil did not possess the political means to prevent school closures and had to move secretly to continue their children's education. Those in Hawaii won legal battles and witnessed the decline of political control which had been enjoyed previously by the white majority in the territory.

Japanese-language schools continued to survive in the postwar era in both Brazil and Hawaii. Few of the third, fourth, or fifth generations of the Japanese-Brazilians and Japanese Americans have communicative skills in Japanese. Children attend Japanese-language schools mostly because they have to. Only the older students are able to make up their own minds, based on what benefits they perceive. Some have decided to attend for cultural rewards and others for what they see as economic benefits.

In the next chapter, I would like to delineate the contemporary situation in the Japanese community in California by focusing on language schools there.

Chapter Seven
Language and Heritage Maintenance Efforts During and After World War II

Mrs. I. Kagawa, a Nisei: "The Nisei, we over-did Americaniza-
tion. Everything goes with the times. We change. Like I said, if I
thought Japanese language was going to be so useful, I would have
sent the children on to Japanese school too but . . . I didn't know."
—David Mas Matsumoto, *Country Voices: The Oral History*
of a Japanese American Family Farm Community (1987)

Japanese-language schools in California and Hawaii all closed with
the outbreak of war between the United States and Japan. School
principals and teachers were among the first Japanese arrested by the
FBI and interned. Many parents and teachers alike burned or discarded Japanese language books, including Japanese-language school
textbooks and materials, for fear of being suspected as pro-Japanese
nationalists when questioned by the FBI. Children, young as they
were, innocently rejoiced at the sudden closure of the Japanese-language schools.

To ascertain educational conditions among Nisei during World
War II, we need to conduct substantially more research, especially
by utilizing available Japanese resources. However, one publication
by Thomas James concerning the overall schooling of Japanese Americans during this period provides us with a previously undisclosed
picture of what happened inside relocation camps. In his discussion
of the educational experiences of Japanese Americans from 1942 to
1945, James refers to Japanese-language schools at Tule Lake Segregation Center, a camp for "disloyals." The people were considered
"disloyal" to the American government because they answered "no"
to these questions: "Are you willing to serve in the armed forces of

the United States on combat duty, wherever ordered?" and "Will you swear unqualified allegiance to the United States of America and faithfully defend the United States from any or all attacks by foreign or domestic forces, and forswear any form of allegiance or obedience to the Japanese Emperor or any other foreign government, power or organization?" At Tule Lake, teachers at public schools refused to administer the loyalty test on the grounds that they felt that such procedures were excessive. After this controversy over loyalty testing, public schooling was made no longer compulsory at the camp. The authorities were surprised to find that in all ten camps, more than a fourth of all Nisei males of draft age did not answer "yes" to the allegiance question. That did not mean that those Nisei, called "no-no-boys," showed loyalty to Japan, but they simply could not support the country unconditionally because they felt the way questions were raised was not right and the manner in which they were treated was not what they expected of American democracy.[1]

James reports that by the fall of 1944, roughly 4,300 students were enrolled in Japanese-language schools at Tule Lake, while only 2,300 students attended the War Relocation Authority's (WRA) public schools. He concludes that these officially condoned language schools at Tule Lake were "an expanded version of the Japanese cultural activities permitted by WRA on a smaller scale in all of the camps."[2]

There was one very nationalistic Japanese-language school in the camp, however. This particular school tried to imitate as closely as possible the Kokumin Gakko, the national elementary school system of Japan in the 1930s. Teachers emphasized discipline, conformity, and respect for superiors. Although younger children seemed to like this uncommonly idealistic school, the high school students tended to prefer WRA's public schools because of their freedom and respect for individual development. All in all, however, James concludes that "for the majority of children in the camp, a Japanese cultural education was not for future life in Japan; it was to satisfy parental wishes that they affirm their Japanese heritage, irrespective of where they went after the war."[3]

After the end of World War II, it took a few years for Issei to reestablish their community mother-tongue schools. In Los Angeles, for instance, Rafu Dai-ichi Gakuen, which was originally established in 1911 as Rafu Nihonjin Gakuen, reopened its doors in February 1949 as part of the Nihongo Gakuen system in Southern California. Though much smaller in number compared to the prewar period, new immigrants from Japan started coming to the United States, and the children of these *Shin-Issei* (new-Issei) enrolled in the re-opened Japanese-language schools. They tried to maintain the Japanese-language ability of their children by sending them to these schools.

When talk of the Era of the Pacific was revived in the 1980s, interest in Japan's language and culture surged in Pacific Rim nations as well as other parts of the world. Calls to utilize the third- and fourth-generation Japanese Americans as a "bridge of understanding" between the two nations are, however, scarcely heard from either the American or Japanese side. One needs to acquire full communicative competence, and language instruction in present Japanese-language schools is a far cry from answering such needs. Limited hours of instruction, inadequate salaries for teachers, and a lack of motivation on the part of students are among the problems cited by today's language-school administrators and teachers. Of course, these adverse conditions are not new. The prewar period faced similar challenges but offered enough incentives and rewards to create an increasing number of schools.

There have been some positive changes, however. Many public high schools in California now accept credits from private foreign language schools. The provision of Section 7511 of the California Education Code enacted in 1963 pursuant to the provisions of Assembly Bill 1800 (1963 session) provides for credit for the foreign-language requirements of the public schools of private language-school courses to meet the minimum standards for such courses in the public schools grades six through junior college.[4] However, Japanese was not included among the officially recognized foreign-languages in high schools, and thus the provisions were not applied to Japanese-language schools. To rectify this imbalance, Assemblymen Edward E. Elliott and Charles Warren introduced Assembly Bill 202, which was approved by the Assembly Education Committee on April 29, 1965.[5] This immediate reward for students has helped them remain in private schools until junior high school or even high school. Yet overall enrollment in Japanese-language schools is much smaller than that of the prewar period.

In this chapter, a survey conducted at a Japanese-language school in Los Angeles will be discussed in order to reveal demographic and attitudinal aspects of the contemporary language schools. The chapter also covers ethnographic research conducted at a language school in Los Angeles. Furthermore, it will deal with a new type of Japanese school for so-called Japanese returning children, *Kikokushijo*, who expect to reside temporarily in the United States and return to Japan with their parents.

Survey of a Japanese-Language School

David Lopez, in his resource book on language maintenance and the language shift situations of different ethnolinguistic communities in the United States today, refers to the relatively low population increase of Japanese Americans (the population increase of Japanese Americans from 1970 to 1980 was only 18.5 percent, compared to 85 percent and 126 percent for Chinese and Filipino groups, respectively). Lopez concludes that the Japanese in the United States are no longer a language minority. And "certainly there is no hope for the English mother-tongue Sansei (third-generation) to use Japanese. However much they might like to 'return' to their culture, they will not do it though their ethnic language."[6]

Fishman reports that there were 142 Japanese-community mother-tongue schools in the United States as of 1979, with 62 schools in Hawaii, 49 in California, and 26 in other states.[7] Some of these schools are for the children born to Japanese Americans, whereas others are for the children of Japanese nationals residing in the United States temporarily. The latter schools are called *Nihonjin Gakko* (Japanese schools), and some of them are *Zen'nichisei-ko* (all-day schools) and others are *Hoshu-ko* (supplementary schools) operated only on Saturdays. These schools receive financial support from the Japanese government.

Locations of Japanese-community schools are of interest. They are concentrated in California and Hawaii but are also scattered throughout the nation. The states where such schools can be found are the following: Massachusetts (1), New York (8), New Jersey (2), Ohio (2), Illinois (4), Michigan (2), District of Columbia (1), Mississippi (1), Louisiana (1), Texas (2), Washington (1), Oregon (1), Alaska (3), and Guam (1).

Fishman, in other research, studied teachers' and students' perceptions of the language schools. He reports that the teachers of the language schools were not positive about the possibility of language maintenance through their schools. The students, on the other hand, seem to be more direct in expressing feelings about schools. They tend to "wonder why they need to learn that language anyway, what use it can possibly be to them, and what others will think of them for knowing it."[8] This kind of negative attitude among the students toward the language schools seems to be prevalent across ethnic lines.

In California, there are two Japanese-language school associations. One is Kashu Nihongo Gakuen Kyokai (California Association of Japanese Language Schools, Inc.) and the other is Beikoku Nihongo Gakko Renmei (the Japanese Language Association of America). The former consists of five northern California branch schools, nine Bay Area branch schools, and nineteen southern California branch schools. One of the major purposes of the former association lies in its authority to give examinations for foreign-language credits in public schools.

The tests examine students' language skills in reading, spelling, writing, composition, conversation, or "any other subject the State Authority or local school district shall prescribe for such tests."[9] The association then reports the results of the tests to the principals of respective public schools and the local board of education for credit consideration. With this accrediting system, students do not need to worry about why they are coming to Japanese-language schools on Saturdays.

The 1989 edition of the *Southern California Japanese Telephone Directory & Guide* lists twenty-five Japanese-language schools in Los Angeles and its vicinity. Although the decrease in Japanese-language schools compared to the prewar period is apparent, as Fishman and Markman point out, "given their indecent treatment by the American government during World War II, Japanese Americans miraculously wasted no time snapping back."[10] They also refer to the Japanese Language School Unified System in Los Angeles, commonly known as the Kyodo System, as "one of the most noteworthy networks of these schools on the mainland."[11]

The Kyodo System was founded by Yaemitsu Sugimachi in 1951. Sugimachi opened Rafu Dai-ichi Gakuen in 1948, one of the first

Japanese-language schools in the postwar period, and then gradually incorporated other schools in the Los Angeles area. Scattered throughout Los Angeles, Orange, and Riverside counties, these nine schools became affiliated as the Kyodo System in 1967.

The Junior High School Department (*Chugaku-bu*) was created in 1953 and the Senior High School Department (*Koto-bu*) was established in 1957 right after the first Junior High School Department graduated its first students. As of 1989, the Kyoto System included nine schools consisting of elementary, junior and senior high, *Kyoyo-ka* (culture classes for flower arrangement, calligraphy, tea ceremony, and doll making) and *Kenkyu-bu* (junior college) sections with 80 teachers and total enrollment of approximately 1,300. While the school system is under the guidance of one principal, each branch school has its own parental organization monitoring facilities and policies. The system's Board of Trustees oversees and guides the financial affairs of each school.[12]

In order to gather general demographic data and attitudinal information from students and parents, the following survey was conducted at a junior high and high school in the Kyodo System.[13] Subjects who answered the questionnaire in this survey include 164 junior high and high school students (75 percent of the total) and 215 parents (49 percent of the total). The student questionnaire was carried out in twelve classrooms from seventh through twelfh grades. The parent questionnaire, designed to question both parents of each family, was taken home by the students.

The questionnaire for students consisted of demographic information (place of birth), language use at home (to what degree, with whom), language skills (a self-evaluation of listening, speaking, reading and writing abilities), reasons for attending, and personal opinions about the school. The questionnaire for parents included questions about age, place of birth and occupation, language use at home and work, language skills (a self-evaluation of listening, speaking, reading, and writing abilities), reasons for having children attend the school, and personal opinions about the school. The questionnaires for students and parents were written in both English and Japanese.

Results showed that over 80 percent of students were born in the United States, while only 33.4 percent of the fathers and 11.2

percent of the mothers were U.S.-born citizens. Seventy percent of the fathers used Japanese at work, indicating that they had found a niche for themselves in areas where Japanese is the dominant language. The majority of mothers considered their Japanese linguistic abilities to be as good as native speakers. In contrast to their parents, 20.8 percent of students felt that their listening skills were as good as native speakers while only 6.4 percent were confident enough to claim that their writing skills were at that level.

In terms of attitudes toward the benefits of studying Japanese, the following responses received a high percentage of strong agreement from students: credit-getting (59.1 percent), job opportunity (54.7 percent), helpful when visiting Japan (50.4 percent). Items receiving a low percentage of strong agreement included: providing parents with a social gathering place (4.3 percent), becoming a bridge between the United States and Japan (17.3 percent), and having Japanese American friends (22.4 percent).

Parents indicated somewhat different reasons for having their children attend the schools. The majority of fathers and mothers wanted a cultural and traditional learning experience for their children, although they also hoped that their children's learning Japanese would lead to better employment opportunities.

Overall, the children were more pragmatically oriented and parents focused more on the cultural aspects of learning. The teaching of Japanese today can be considered foreign-language teaching, rather than preparatory language or culture education for the children's return to Japan. Some Japanese-language schools may still remain centers of the local Japanese community. Others can no longer claim to be such. Certainly, very little nationalistic influence can be found in today's language schools.

Observations of Japanese-Language Schools in Los Angeles

To confirm the results of the survey and further fill in the gaps in it, ethnographic research was conducted by visiting two smaller-scale Japanese-language schools in Los Angeles in January and February of 1986. Observation sites were A Gakuen (pseudonym) and B Gakuen (pseudonym).

A Gakuen was established in 1925 with four pupils. The school was temporarily closed between 1941 and 1948 due to World War

II, during which period the school property was under the jurisdiction of the American Red Cross. The enrollment of the school went up to 40 at one time in the prewar period. Between 1950 and 1985, the enrollment was relatively consistent, with an average of 165 students a year.

School is held from 3:00 P.M. to 5:30 P.M., Monday through Friday, and 9:00 A.M. to 12:00 P.M. on Saturdays. The school buildings (four classrooms and one auditorium, of which the capacity is approximately 650 people) are used not only for language instruction but also for such classes as judo, karate, flower arrangement, and Japanese dancing, most of which are traditional Japanese culture-awareness exercises. These different types of classes are held at various periods when classrooms are not being used for language instruction.

A Gakuen

It is not unusual in Japanese schools for teachers or even the school principal to have other jobs and to be teaching part-time. This was the case with A Gakuen as well. The principal turned out to be a chef at a Japanese restaurant. The principal was cleaning up the rooms with a broom and dustpan at the time the observation started.

Three rectangular-shaped rooms and one big hall are used as classrooms. The third-grade children in Room #2 were observed. The class was being taught by the principal. There were fewer than 30 seats in the classroom, which was made up of three rows horizontally facing the blackboard. I was sitting at the right corner of the third row.

Boys and girls form their own groups. For instance, the second row consists of only boys. Whether this is a universal tendency or culture-specific is not clear. At 2:50 P.M., one boy arrived and was greeted by the principal, who noted that the boy had come earlier than usual. Children came in by twos and threes, and most of them noticed my presence, but they soon went out to the playground to engage in various types of play. The majority of the boys on the playground were playing basketball, while girls remained in the classroom chatting or doing something on their own. One of the girls was folding colored papers in accord with a traditional Japanese paper craft, origami. The girl continued to engage in the activity throughout the class period. At 3:10 P.M., the bell rang. Almost all of the children rushed into the classroom, while the two still on the playground were attempting to put a basketball into the basket. Recognizing that the principal was on his way to the classroom, the two boys stopped their game and dashed into the classroom.

At 3:15 P.M., the class started with the principal's command, "Kiritsu, kiotsuke!" (Stand straight up and at attention!). The children stood up all together and then said, "Sensei, kon'nichiwa" (Hello, teacher). Such a scene is rather typical in Japan, and yet their routine surprised me. The children sat down. "What day is it today?" the principal asked everyone in Japanese. No quick answer was given. Some said "suiyobi," or Wednesday, perhaps meaning "Friday." The principal pointed to another child, "Yamada-san, kyo wa nan'yobi desuka?" (Miss Yamada, what day is it today?) "Wasureta," (I forget) she replied. Since no one else seemed to be able to give him a correct answer, the principal wrote a sentence in Japanese on the board: "Kyo wa kin'yobi desu" (Today is Friday). As the principal wrote down the sentence, some of the children were reading what had been written on the board. The children chorally repeated the sentence after the teacher. The teacher then gave out mimeographed sheets to the children for a new lesson. One boy was scolded by the principal for chewing gum.

"What do you say when you get up in the morning?" the principal asked the class. "Ohayo gozaimasu" (Good morning) the class quickly responded. "How about daytime?" "How about at night?" It seemed that everyone knew the answer. The principal explained that in Japanese one had to be careful to use different types of greeting expressions, depending on whom he or she is greeting. The lesson proceeded to the use of sentence patterns using the previously distributed sheets. These sheets contained several pictures, such as an umbrella, a chair, a pen, a book, a cat, a door, an alarm clock, and a notebook. Some of these are English loanwords in Japanese, and thus the principal taught the correct pronunciation and orthographical representation of each of the loanwords that needed to be explained. After covering the items listed on the sheet, the principal asked the children to name some of the items in the classroom, such as a piece of chalk, a window, and the door, and to apply the items to the sentence just learned: "Kore was nan desuka?" (What is this?), "Sore wa . . . desu." (That is . . .). After the pattern practice was conducted, the teacher then assigned homework to the children. At 3:57 p.m., the class ended with the principal's command: "Kiotsuke, rei!" (Attention, bow!).

Every child but two, who had questions for the principal, left the classroom quickly. Soon another group came in. These students were much older than the previous class, perhaps junior high school level. Many of them stayed inside the classroom. Some girls were showing accessories that they had brought into the classroom; others were just chatting with each other.

On the window was a sign that said "Let's all greet each other—this week's target" both in English and Japanese. The noise level was very high. It sounded as though everyone was chatting, screaming, and calling each other's names in English. At least, there were none who was greeting in Japanese.

The bell rang at 4:10 P.M. Every student went back to his/her seat, but they kept chatting. The principal came in. Everyone stood up. Then someone commanded "Rei" (Bow), so they all bowed and sat down. Eight out of nine students in the front row were male students, three out of four in the second row were female students, and the last row consisted of seven female students. It was also interesting to find that there were one or two students in class who sat alone, with no one next to them. This was the case in the third-grade class, too. However, there was a difference between the child in the third-grade class who sat alone and the one in the junior high class. While the former was a very quiet and seemingly docile child, the latter was the exact opposite. He was a stocky, athletic type and a very articulate student. He even walked to the front of the room in the middle of class and pointed out the boy who had thrown a fragment of a rubber eraser at him, accusing him and complaining about it to the principal.

At the beginning of the class, the principal told the students that they should be quiet that day because there was a visitor observing them. It was already easy to predict that this class would be quite different from the third-grade class. The principal started with a review of the previous lesson on greeting. "Minasan kon'nichiwa" (Hello, everyone), the principal said. The class repeated the principal chorally. The lesson consisted of several other greeting expressions. The class was divided into small groups and then pairs. They were to practice the greeting expressions. However, the majority of the class seemed to be committed to other things. The noise level was constantly high. The principal scolded the class several times, individually and collectively. Each time he did, the volume of his voice increased. Finally, at the end of the period, he scolded the students by saying that if they did not want to participate in the class, they did not have to come to the school, and that they should think of their parents who were paying extra money for this school in addition to the regular public school that they attend. After scolding them, the principal told them that what they were learning would not be a wasteful exercise but would be a very useful commodity in their future.

The class ended with a routine: "Kiritsu, rei, sensei sayonara" (Arise, bow, good-bye teacher). The principal told me that this was the most difficult class in this school. Everyone left the school quickly. Some of the students seemed to hurry away to a bus stop.

Teachers at A Gakuen

On the first day of observation at the site, it was possible to meet all the teachers of the school who teach on Saturdays. Except for the principal, all the other five teachers were relatively young, female teachers. Four of the five teachers teach only on Saturdays.

Teacher "A" graduated from UCLA with a major in psychology and is currently enrolled in the M.A. program at California State University at Northridge. Her English was very good, which tended to cause excessive use of it during the class hours. She was in charge of the fifth- and sixth-grade pupils.

Teacher "B," whose Japanese accent reminded me of those in the northern area of Japan, was perhaps the most energetic and oftentimes aggressive teacher in this school. It seemed that she had been in the United States for a while, considering her ability in spoken English. Because of this ability, she also tended to use English excessively in class. "You guys, be quiet, OK?," she said to the class one time. On her behalf, it should be noted that at the time there was good reason for her to call out in this manner. While observing this junior-high class, I encountered a student who suddenly stood up from his desk, walked to Teacher "B" to say something, and then on his way back to his seat said to me, "This is a bad example, huh?" pointing to the teacher.

Teacher "C" came from Tokyo, had been in the United States for three years, and lived in Van Nuys. Along with one other teacher and the school principal, she taught classes six days a week, Mondays through Saturdays. Although Teacher "C" did not have teaching experience while in Japan, her class was well organized and thus her students seemed to follow her instructions. It should be noted that other factors appeared to enhance the concentration and behavior of this teacher's class, including an ideally sized classroom and a relatively docile age group (The younger the student is, the better his or her behavior seemed to be). Also, some of the teachers have to manage under apparently undesirable circumstances, that is, a classroom that has been made by temporarily curtaining off an area of the auditorium. So far as I observed, these more satisfactory conditions helped Teacher "C" with the management of her class.

Teacher "D," a middle-aged, typical Japanese mother–type teacher was, according to the principal, a veteran teacher in this school. She taught only on weekdays. She was the only teacher who controlled the students' seating arrangement, which seemed to be an important factor for class management, and she was also the only teacher in the school who walked around the classroom enough to maintain the students' attentiveness to the lesson. Most of the other teachers had a tendency to go to particular students only for the purpose of warning them to behave well in the classroom. Teacher "D" taught the first-grade and high school–level students on weekdays.

As far as two other teachers are concerned, I did not obtain much information except that both of them were relative newcomers who did not seem to have a positive image of the school management or of their own roles in the school.

Interviews with Teachers
Teacher "D"
An interview with Teacher "D" was conducted in her classroom. She pulled out some data used for the creation of the survey and began to talk about what had motivated her to have the students conduct the surveys. "There was, as far as I heard from the previous school princi-

pal, a big celebration held at the school in commemoration of its fiftieth year of establishment. Therefore, the school was not preparing much for the sixtieth anniversary celebration. However, the previous school principal suddenly resigned last September and the present principal succeeded him. Because of this occasion, the school decided to celebrate the sixtieth anniversary on the same scale as they had for the fiftieth anniversary. I was given responsibility for exhibits to be shown on Establishment Day in November of last year. I wondered what would be the best exhibits for such a big event as this when the city mayor and consul of Japan are expected to come. I came to the conclusion that the exhibition of survey results which introduces the school's history and the present configuration of the school, such as the students' ethnic background and generational differences, would appeal to the audience. This was the driving force that motivated me to have my students work on the surveys."

"The result of the survey was based on the twenty years between 1950 and 1970, therefore, I am not sure about what happened after that time," she said. "Nevertheless," she continued, "I think it is safe to say that the trend of enrollment may be slightly up or down, but for the most part it remains even." "The price of land and housing have been increasing in this area," Teacher "D" stated. "It is difficult for a young couple with one or two children to come into this residential area, as I understand it. That may be one factor which prevents the younger generation from sending their children to this school." "Another Japanese school that I know of is a somewhat different case," she went on to say, "It is located near downtown Los Angeles and the area surrounding the school has become quite a dangerous place in which to live. There are many crimes and so forth, and because of this, the enrollment figures have been decreasing at the school. However, there is a positive factor which I think is contributing to the enrollment in this school: An increasing number of Caucasian children have been signing up recently."

"About two days ago," she changed the subject, "I read an article pertaining to a survey which inquired about the importance people place on learning a foreign language. The outcome of the survey was very interesting. Over 80 percent of those surveyed answered that learning a foreign language is important, especially so when one is still young. This kind of result is very encouraging for us. I hope we can contribute to this positive trend one way or another. However, I would also like to add that many of the children of non-Japanese parents seem to drop out as the semester progresses, perhaps because there is little chance for them to practice Japanese except when they are in school. I also notice that occasionally parents are frustrated at meetings where the agenda is discussed in Japanese."

Teacher "D" went on to say, "The last five years, it seems that the population learning Japanese has been rapidly increasing. I understand that UCLA has some very big Japanese classes and also that some schools on the East Coast include the Japanese language in their curriculum. What some people call "Japanese fever" may also be a motivating factor in the maintenance of the enrollment in our school."

"I usually have several students at my home as home-stay students from Japan," she said. "Looking at these students, I am convinced that no matter how long they stay in the United States, they find Japanese friends more comfortable to get along with than American friends. This is not to say that they do not make American friends at all. I just wish to point out that there is a general tendency among Japanese students to flock together. The same thing seems to apply to the students here. Even though they say that they have a lot of American friends, they seem to be pretty comfortable chatting with their Japanese friends at a Japanese school."

"By the way," she interjected, "there is one thing that I just recalled now. I have a friend who is teaching law at UCLA. He belongs to the same church that I do. One day, when we were casually talking to each other, he told me that he is rather envious of me. I asked him why and he told me that it was because I could directly face Caucasians with my broken English without any hesitancy. He said that he could not do it. So I asked him why this was the case, despite his social status and intelligence, and above all his native skills in English. He confessed to me that when he was a child, he was in one of the concentration camps. He saw that his mother was afraid of the Caucasians and he behaved likewise. He heard the white people constantly calling his parents 'Jap, Jap.' This negative image of his identity as a Japanese is always in his mind whenever he faces Caucasians. He also told me that he was envious of Japanese businessmen who go to luxurious restaurants and conduct business on equal terms. He said he just couldn't do that sort of things. I was very shocked by his confession."

Teacher "D" then went on to talk about the fact that many of the immigrants from Japan possessed considerable social status, in spite of a general impression people have that most of them are poor farmers. She described how grateful she is to have been given a chance to get to know the students; that when she returned to Japan every year, she took some of her students along and they lived together there for about three weeks; and that those students always express their desire to attend college in Japan.

Teacher "C"

Teacher "C" started by saying "I was looking for this type of job when I came to the United States with my husband. In the advertising section of the *Rafu Shimpo* I found that this school had a job opening for a teacher. I applied for the job and was accepted. I have been working just six months." She went on to say, "I don't know if you realize this, but, with the exception of Teacher "D" and the principal, all the teachers in this school are relatively newly hired. Teacher "A" and myself are the newest teachers here." Regarding the difference between the image that she had had of this teaching job and the reality that she faced, she said, "I was expecting that this school would be more like a *juku* (after-school 'cram school') in Japan, the kind that education-minded mothers in Japan are earnest about sending their children to. So my expectation of the children was quite high. I was anticipating a group of children, highly motivated to learning Japanese language and culture. However, what I found here was quite the opposite. It seems that the majority of the children come to this school because their parents wish them to. I was rather surprised to find how noisy they are during class hours. I teach both weekdays and Saturday classes. Usually the weekday classes are quieter and better behaved than their Saturday counterpart. However, as far as my classes are concerned, the opposite is true. I have hard-working students in the Saturday classes, but I don't know why."

Although she was rather disappointed by the fact that the students were much less motivated and less disciplined than she had thought they would be, she was still interested in teaching there for a while. She said, "Yes, I will, at least for a while. The time schedule of this school fits well in my schedule." She continued, "I've been getting ten dollars per hour. That's not too bad for me. But, that isn't enough for a male teacher who has a family of his own. That's why, I guess, there are no male teachers in this school. You know, even the principal has a second job."

"What I wish my students would do," she continued, "is to speak in Japanese as much as possible. In class they seem to ask most of their questions in English. However, I usually answer them in Japanese. There is one student, one of the brothers of non-Japanese speaking parents, who doesn't understand what I am saying at all. A major problem that I have in my classes is that the levels of Japanese language skills among the students in one class vary dramatically. There are some students who are very fluent in Japanese, but there are others who cannot even understand what I am explaining to them in Japanese. It seems that there are no middle-level students. I hate to bore the good students, but at the same time I cannot leave the rest of them always lagging behind. I have to tell you at this point that whether or not one's parents are speaking Japanese at home does not necessarily decide the student's achievement at this school. In the brothers' case that I am talking about, one of them is lagging behind, while the other is a good student and is doing very well." Concerning other problems she has with this school, she pointed out the lack of proper teaching materials and scarcity of appropriate advice. "I was expecting to receive some advice from other teachers as to how to cope with various problems, but I've never been taught how to teach the children in this school."

In short, most of the comments from Teacher "C" were rather negative. She seemed to be still struggling with the system and her relationship with other teachers as well as students. Lack of teaching experience and the gap between what she had expected and the reality kept bothering her. She might well have provided a totally different opinion several years later, but all the problems she pointed out can be shared by the majority of the teachers in Japanese-language schools. The same can probably be said of some of the language schools in the prewar period.

Parents

I was not allowed to interview parents of A Gakuen. However, there were a few opportunities to observe parents at the school. One Saturday, in one of the classes which was being held in a corner of the school auditorium, a couple of mothers walked across the classroom, carrying plastic containers that appeared to be used for cooking. It was almost noon and a good aroma was wafting from a kitchen next door. A number of mothers were busy preparing a big dinner for a special occasion for their children's judo club. This abrupt appearance of the mothers and such an inviting smell in the classroom were naturally accepted by the class. It was as though such interruptions were business as usual.

At the end of the class, parents would come to school to pick up their children and chat with the teachers. Most of the topics had to do with the children's behavior at school. In other words, the parents' expectations of the teachers and the school in general are more related to the amelioration of their children's undesirable behavior in their own homes, than to the acquisition of Japanese-language skills. This assumption should not be applied to the entire population of parents in this school. And yet, it is also true that a number of events could support this assumption.

There are several reasons why parents send their children to the school. The results of the survey at the Kyodo System revealed that parents tended to expect the school to provide their children with cultural and traditional learning experiences. In other words, the parents there expected the language school to play more of a symbolic than a pragmatic role. In the course of observations at this school, it was rather difficult to judge whether the parents sent their children to the school because of pragmatic reasons or symbolic reasons. It may be futile to search for a single motive, since one reason would probably not be enough motivation for the parents to invest in extra education for the children.

In an informal talk with some of the junior-high students, one student said that she used to be eager to learn Japanese, but her study was disturbed by those students who constantly make noise in the classroom. She was also critical of the teachers of this school in general. In fact, some of the teachers themselves, many of whom are relatively newly hired and inexperienced teachers, admitted that they were lacking in knowledge and experience in language teaching.

Is the situation at A Gakuen typical of Japanese-language schools in general or is it a characteristic phenomenon applicable only to A

Gakuen? The general setting, such as limited instructional hours, community-oriented school operations, and children's relatively low motivation in the language learning, do not seem to be tremendously different from one Japanese-language school to another. Differences could be seen in such areas as the experience and knowledge of the teachers, the principal's leadership, the quality of teaching materials, and parental support.

B Gakuen

B Gakuen was created in 1915 by a minister of religion. School is held only on Saturday mornings from 8:45 to 12:15, as is the case with many Japanese-language schools in California. The number of students is approximately 200. There are six classrooms and a hall, which is also used as a classroom. Four of the six classrooms are located in one structure, approximately 20 square meters, the inside of which is divided by wooden accordion-type curtains. Therefore, one can hear the noise in the adjacent rooms, and yet it was not as disruptive as one would imagine.

Teachers in B Gakuen were more experienced than other teachers I observed and therefore handled the students somewhat better. The principal had been working for the school for nearly twenty years and seemed to be well-respected by the teachers and the parents. Thus, the parents appeared to be supportive of the operations of the school. On the observation day, a number of members of the school PTA were busy preparing newsletters in the teachers' staff room. In a casual meeting of the teachers at the end of the school hours, a representative of the PTA was present and gave the impression that such an interaction of the teachers and the parents is not uncommon at this school.

All the teachers observed at B Gakuen, without exception, were anxious to know about what I noticed in my observations of their classes. After the class, the teachers usually asked for comments about their lessons. Those teachers who were not observed even complained about my not observing their classes. Detailed comments on the teachers' teaching strategies will not be discussed here, since further observations would be necessary.

The students of B Gakuen were not much different from those students in A Gakuen. Some students were quiet and rarely volunteered their opinions, while others were quite outspoken and sometimes disturbing for the rest of the class. Students were, in general, relaxed and did not much care about the presence of an observer. In other words, they did not seem to have the slightest intention of pretending that they were good students, although some of them did glance at me occasionally. The majority of the students, according to the school principal, attend the school because their parents wish them to. Therefore, the level of the students' motivation for learning Japanese hardly reaches the degree of the parents' and the teachers' expectations. During the break periods, it is typical for the children to rush out of the classroom and enjoy playing with their peers, and then, reluctantly, return to the classroom at the bell.

The low motivation of the students in learning the Japanese language should not be emphasized excessively, however. Several students were very much enjoying learning Japanese language and culture. In a number of cases the class was lively and almost all the pupils' hands were raised with enthusiasm to answer the teacher's questions. Some students remained at the end of the class to ask questions of the teacher, rather than running around on the playground. Nevertheless, if the pupils were coming to the school not because they want to but because their parents tell them to, and furthermore, since they do not have to come to the school every Saturday, how can one expect the students of the language schools to devote themselves eagerly to the extra work? For the majority of the students, it seemed that finding significance in learning Japanese is not an easy task.

All this being said, why have the Japanese-language schools continued to exist, with fairly consistent enrollment figures maintained for decades? John Edwards, for example, maintains that "language and other visible characteristics can be altered or lost in the face of changing circumstances, without the loss of identity."[14] Based on this assumption, there is not a very good chance for the survival of the ethnic-language schools. Even if they do, in fact, survive, the function of these schools may be altered from mere language instruction to activities of overall ethnic identity preservation.

An Interview with the President of the California Association of Japanese-Language Schools

The president seemed to be aware of this possible crisis for the Japanese-language schools. Yet, he was optimistic about the future of the schools. He quoted a recent study on the effect of bilingualism on the children's cognitive development and also referred to a recent census on the people's opinions about having the children learn a foreign language.

The study he was referring to was conducted by a psycholinguist and reported at a meeting of the American Psychological Association. Based on his research on Spanish-English bilingual children in New Haven, he concluded that bilingual children were better in the skills of problem solving than their English-speaking counterparts. Furthermore, he suggested that forcing English-only instruction on minority children may have a negative effect on their emotional as well as their intellectual development.

Based on this study the president stressed the significance of maintaining, and moreover enhancing, the Japanese-language schools in American society. He was convinced that in order for the United States, as the leading nation of the world, to be understood by the rest of the world, it is imperative that it devote itself to foreign language instruction, and that the Japanese-language schools could contribute to this effort.

He also stressed that Japanese-language schools can play an important role in bilateral relations between Japan and the United States. Two years earlier, he had an opportunity to discuss this matter with some of the representatives of major Japanese multinational corporations. The head of the delegates told him that in order to deepen mutual understanding between the two nations, it is imperative that both nations put their fullest efforts into the education of youngsters who have the potential for manipulating both languages and thus possess deep understanding of both cultures. He continued that Japanese multinational corporations had invested substantial amounts of money in such efforts, whereas it is doubtful that their U.S. counterparts had done the same. Although he admitted that learning English and American culture might have more value and applicability in situations around the world than learning Japanese language and culture, he insisted that Japanese-language schools could compensate for such lack of efforts on the part of American society. Therefore, the schools should function not only to maintain Japanese language and culture among Japanese Americans, but also to foster bilingual individuals who could contribute to a better international relationship.

He also pointed out some of the positive aspects of the schools. For instance, he referred to some Chinese parents who send their children to a certain Japanese-language school, because Japanese-language skills would be a tremendous advantage for future job opportunities. A large number of Chinese students in mainland China study hard in order to obtain a chance to go to Japan for study, for doing so will guarantee them a better salary upon their return to China. Knowing this situation in their motherland, the Chinese parents felt that having their children attend a Japanese-language school with a moderate tuition could place their children in a better position in the future. The president also mentioned that there are other non-Japanese students in some schools, including those of white, black, Jewish, Korean, and Mexican origins. One white female student, who is in the seventh grade, is an honor student at the principal's school. A black father, who is an attorney, had the experience of living in Japan and keenly feels the necessity of getting acquainted with the Japanese language and culture and decided to provide his children with the chance of learning about them in the United States. A Jewish parent once made a speech entitled "Living with Three Different Cultures" at the school. With all these examples, the principal is convinced that the new leaders of the United States should be those who can manipulate languages other than English and possess deep understanding of other cultures. He hopes that these non-Japanese students in Japanese-language schools will be able to contribute to the betterment of international relations in the future. He mentioned that currently 27 students could be classified as non-Japanese among the total enrollment of 1,300 students in the Kyodo System.

The ethnographic data described here was gathered at Japanese-language schools in Los Angeles. However, there are schools of another type for Japanese children in the United States, which we should not overlook. They are Japanese schools established for the purpose of preparing Japanese children returning from the United States for re-entry into the Japanese system.

Contemporary Japanese Schools Abroad

A relatively recent phenomenon, the presence of children of Japanese businessmen has increased at a rapid rate in metropolitan areas throughout the United States. So-called *Kikokushijo* (Japanese returning children) can be defined here as those children who have a certain period of educational experience abroad because of their parents' (mostly fathers') occupational assignments in foreign countries. The parents generally work for trading companies, banks, or the Japanese government. These parents are not immigrants but temporary residents.

The first Japanese overseas school in the postwar era was established in Taipei in 1953; this was soon followed by another school in Bangkok in 1955. The opening of these schools was made possible by the voluntary efforts of parents, with the cooperation of the Overseas Council of Japan. The schools in Taipei and Bangkok were full-time schools, as is more often seen in developing nations. Although there are some full-time Japanese schools in developed nations such as England and the United States, the majority of the children in these nations attend supplementary schools.

As of 1993, there were approximately 51,000 Japanese children of compulsory education age residing in foreign countries, out of which 21,261 are in North America, comprising 41.8 percent of the total.[15] In Los Angeles, for example, there is one all-day school called Kokusai Gakuen (International Bilingual School) in Palos Verdes. Established in 1978, the school consists of a nursery school, elementary school, and junior high school. The academic year begins in April, as is the case in Japan. The school curriculum is based on guidelines set by Mombusho. The school offers not only an English as a Second Language course, but also an English grammar course taught in the same manner as English is taught in Japan.

There are supplementary schools in Los Angeles called Asahi Gakuen, founded by the Association for the Promotion of Japanese Language Education in Los Angeles and financially supported by Nihon Boeki Konwa-kai (the Japan Traders' Club of Los Angeles). Asahi Gakuen had an enrollment of 2,500 students in 1988. Although the majority of teachers are hired locally, those in administrative positions are visiting staff from Japan sent on the recommendation of Mombusho. The school system consists of five branch schools scattered throughout Los Angeles and Orange counties. Classes are held every Saturday from 9:00 A.M. to 3:30 P.M. Subject matter includes Japanese, mathematics, social science and science. The textbooks used are written in Japan. Also, the academic year also begins in April and ends in March, as in Japan.

As the number of Japanese working abroad increases, the educational and social problems involving their children also increase. Problems of returning children have received extensive attention in Japan in recent years, especially in connection with bullying. Returning students' inability to speak proper Japanese and their "foreign" behavior often make them the object of ridicule. In calling them "han japa," or half-Japanese, the "pure" Japanese students treat the returnees mercilessly. A returning child described her experience in Japan in the following way.

When I first went back to Japan, I tried not to talk. I spoke with an American accent, and that seemed funny to people. It's better now, but it's still hard to get along. . . . The girls I met liked different things than my friends in the U.S. And especially at first, I acted more American than Japanese. My teachers still tell me I stand out too much.[16]

However, Roger Goodman suggests that Japanese researchers have focused too emphatically on the negative aspects of the returnees so that "such a negative theme, indeed, has become almost institutionalised in public circles by always referring to the "returnee children problem" (*Kikokushijo Mondai*) which creates the impression that these children either have or are some kind of problem."[17]

This Kikokushijo Mondai reminds us of the *Dai-Nisei Mondai* (the second-generation problems), so frequently discussed among Issei in the prewar Japanese community in America. Second-generation problems included the Niseis' problems with employment, marriage, dual citizenship, and education. All of these were certainly serious problems for the Nisei, which concerned many Issei. Given the frequent use of the word mondai, however, we need to be cautious about its translation. When contemporary Japanese speak of Kikokushijo Mondai, they do not necessarily mean "these children either have or are some kind of problem." The kikokushijo mondai, therefore, might be better translated as "the returning children issue."

In recent years, returnees have come to be seen as precious human resources rather than problem children. In fact, high school returnees, who reach the age of eighteen years and are ready to take college entrance examinations in Japan, are somewhat more privi-

leged than the rest of the high school students in Japan. The returnees in this age bracket can take advantage of special quotas set in a
number of prestigious universities. Some parents even try to send
their children abroad just to utilize this special quota system. Returnees also enjoy better chances of being employed by big firms,
for large corporations need people with good language skills. Of
course, not everything is rosy for returnees, but the situation is im-
proving for those who could have been rejected by society a few
years earlier.

Epilogue
Beyond Language and Cultural Barriers

*Just as the classroom is not where learning starts, it is not where it
ends either.*
> —Verónica Cortínez, "The Excitement of Literature:
> A Lifelong Pursuit," in Wilga Rivers, ed.,
> *Teaching Languages in College:
> Curriculum and Content* (1992)

As Joshua Fishman points out, two mutually exclusive forces—language maintenance and language shift—coexist in different sets of time and space and are ever-fluctuating processes, both on individual and social levels. Historically, the growth of public education, mass culture, a more open system of politics, and economic as well as social rewards for English speakers in the United States has accelerated the immigrants' language shift.[1]

On November 12, 1985, in Monterey Park, California, a topic on the agenda of a meeting of the City Council attracted a great deal of public attention. It was about whether or not the city should make English its official language. About the half of the city's population consists of people of Asian origins. Many store signs are written in languages virtually unintelligible to non-immigrant, English-speaking citizens. Frank Arcuri, one of the original advocates of the idea of proclaiming English as the official language of the city, declared that he had obtained the approval of 72 percent of the registered voters of Monterey Park, one-third of them Asians. Furthermore, he pointed out that a substantial portion of the Asian signers consisted of Japanese Americans. Japanese Americans, according to him, agreed with his idea because they are "super Americans."

This particular incident, which is by no means the first of its kind, reflects the current language shift and language maintenance phenomena in the United States. The story is also interesting in that Japanese Americans are looked upon as people of assimilationist orientation. In fact, Japanese Americans are generally viewed to have adapted to American values and ethics better than many other non-white immigrants, despite their cultural differences and the discrimination they have experienced. It has even been said that one can "scratch a Japanese American and find a white Anglo-Saxon Protestant."[2] Thus they tend to be looked at as a "model minority" and their success stories are prevalent. Of course, those Japanese who do not consider themselves as successful as they are often described think that they have been used to calm down vocal and demanding minorities.

Granted that Japanese Americans have adapted—or at least attempted to adapt—to American values and ethics, does this mean that the continuation of this cultural adaptation may result in the total elimination of the ethnic community as well as of their ancestral language in the future? Although it appears that language maintenance efforts among Japanese Americans have been relatively unsuccessful, such efforts have always existed and are continuing at present.

I have attempted to observe language and heritage maintenance efforts of Japanese Americans and to a lesser extent other cases involving Japanese and other ethnic minorities, from their past experience to the present. As mentioned earlier, in 1912 Japanese educators in California held a meeting in San Francisco concerned with the teaching of the Japanese language to the American-born children of Japanese ancestry. At their meeting, they resolved that "all children born in America should be educated in American public schools to be able to live their lives in this country." Japanese-language schools were able to justify their existence only by limiting their roles to supplementary education for the American-born children. It may appear that the aim of the language schools at the early stage was oriented toward assimilation. Despite orientation of the institutions to Americanization, Japanese-language schools were the object of anti-Japanese agitation in California and Hawaii. Similar accusations were applied to Japanese immigrants in Brazil. They were constantly charged with being a menace to mainstream ideals. Teaching languages other than English (or Portuguese in Brazil) was felt to run counter to the process of the children's assimilation. The ostensible assimilation orientation of the early Japanese immigrants was not inherent, but rather was an outcome resulting from external pressures. As a matter of survival, Issei educators needed to demonstrate their loyalty to the host societies.

As third- and fourth-generation Japanese Americans are integrated into American society, the Japanese language has diminished in significance within the Japanese-American community. The development of language skills for second-generation children has been successful only for a few. In addition, the development of Japanese-language schools was affected by changes in society. Anti-Oriental sentiment in the early twentieth century, the Americanization movement in the 1920s, the Great Depression, and deteriorating U.S.-Japan relations in the late 1930s were major social, economic, and political factors that influenced not only the development of Japanese-language schools but all spheres of life for the immigrants. Public schools also played a role as agents for the Americanization movement, thereby strongly affecting the thoughts and behavior of Nisei. Issei had ambivalent feelings about the public schools. While they were institutions that provided pride because of the achievement of Nisei, they were intermediaries that distanced their children.

However, I want to emphasize that the schools played a significant role in satisfying the needs of the immigrant community across generational differences. Under the adverse circumstances mentioned above, Japanese-language schools did function as community centers for the immigrants. Child care, communication with the children, comfort through socialization with other parents, having their children avoid "street" influences, participating in a community center, and fulfilling patriotic obligations toward Japan were among the benefits that Issei particularly enjoyed.

After traumatic and yet culturally enriching experiences in isolated camps in the desert during World War II, Japanese immigrants re-established language schools to serve mainly the children of newly arrived *Shin-Issei* (new-Issei). Another development in contemporary community schools among Japanese in the United States is the formation of such schools as Nihonjin Gakko and Hoshu-ko for the children of Japanese nationals. The Japanese language remains alive in diversified community schools while the new breed of Japanese immigrants and other temporary residents continue to knock on the doors of public schools.

"[I]t is almost as if there were an unspoken national policy to do whatever is necessary to deny opportunities for the conservation of the competencies held by these linguistic minority students," Campbell and Lindholm observed. However, they also point out that language maintenance efforts can be witnessed even on government and state levels where efforts have been made to promote the awareness of ethnic mother tongue maintenance as a national resource.[3] While the English Language Amendment has kept pressure on language minority groups, an increasing number of universities and colleges ask students to finish foreign-language requirements for graduation.[4]

English has become today's international auxiliary language. Therefore, the rewards for knowing English usually far exceed those of being able to speak Japanese and any other language. Given the perceived growing economic rewards to be found in learning Japanese, however, efforts to maintain the Japanese language and cultural heritage in the United States and elsewhere are sure to continue.

Appendices

Place	Schools	Teachers	Pupils
San Francisco	3	9	160
Alameda	3	5	54
Vacaville	1	1	8
Sacramento	5	7	142
Stockton	1	1	17
Fresno	1	2	48
Watsonville	1	1	57
San Jose	3	6	102
So. California	10	12	128
Total	28	44	716

Source: Zaibei Nihonjin-kai Jiseki Hozonbu, *Zaibei Nihonjin-shi* [A History of Japanese in the United States]. (1940).

Appendix B Japanese-Language Schools in California as of 1940*

Table B-1. Northern/Central California

School	Teachers	Students	Established
Nihon Gakuen	2	51	1902
Penlin Nihongo Gakuen	3	141	1902
Sakura Gakuen	10	480	1903
Alviso Nihongo Gakuen	1	15	1905
Fu-shi Nihongo Gakuen	6	211	1905
A-shi Gakuen	1	33	1907
Sa-shi Nihongo Gakuen	2	70	1907
Mii Gakuen	1	20	1908
Su-shi Gakuen	7	275	1908
Agnew Nihongo Gakuen	1	22	1910
Showa Gakuen	3	95	1910
Wanto Gakuen	4	130	1910

School	Teachers	Students	Established
Kings-gun Jido Kyoikukai	2	60	1911
Kinmon Gakuen	8	465	1911
Armona Hoshu Gakuen	2	25	1912
Berryessa Nihongo Gakuen	2	39	1912
Canal Gakuen	2	23	1912
Isleton Gakuen	2	132	1912
Kawashimo Gakuen	3	145	1912
Bakuryo Nihongo Gakko	2	30	1913
Church Gakuen	2	52	1913
Florin Mii Kyokai Fuzoku Gakuen	2	60	1913
Kason Gakuen	3	150	1913
Taisho Gakuen	2	50	1913
Gyosei Gakuen	9	215	1914
Kyowa Gakuen	1	40	1914
Marysville Gakuen	4	230	1914
Yoro Gakuen	1	35	1914
Mountainview Nihongo Gakuen	2	70	1915
Roa Gakuen	2	86	1915
Alameda Gakuen	4	148	1916
Courtland Nihongo Gakuen	2	37	1916
Fresno Gakuen	2	42	1916
Los Gatos Nihongo Gakuen	1	21	1916
Monterey Kokugo Gakuen	2	60	1916
New Castle Nihongo Gakuen	2	78	1916
San Mateo Nihongo Gakuen	2	73	1916
Fowler Nihongo Gakuen	3	125	1917
Selma Nihongo Gakuen	3	117	1917
Del Rey Nihongo Gakuen	3	95	1918
Hokubu Gakuen	1	58	1918
Kahan Nihongo Gakuen	2	32	1918
Mayfield Nihongo Gakuen	2	30	1918
Colusa Gakuen	1	60	1920
Florin Bukkyo shozoku- Nihongo Gakuen	3	112	1920
Alvarado Gakuen	2	35	1922
Edenville Nihongo Gakuen	1	35	1923
Gilroy Nihongo Gakuen	1	102	1923
Madera Nihongo Gakuen	2	61	1923
Blackstone Gakuen	1	20	1924
Elder Creek Nihongo Gakuen	2	42	1924
Monterey Kirisutokyo Gakuen	1	40	1924
Redwood Nihongo Gakuen	1	32	1924

School	Teachers	Students	Established
Reedley Nihongo Gakuen	4	182	1924
Salinas Nihongo Gakuen	2	100	1924
Soko Gakuen	6	250	1924
Belmont Gakuen	1	22	1925
Biola Nihongo Gakuen	2	40	1925
Centerville Gakuen	1	46	1925
Delano Nihongo Gakuen	2	140	1925
Eden Gakuen	1	40	1925
Menlo Park Nihongo Gakuen	2	14	1925
Palo Alto Nihongo Gakuen	2	20	1925
Petaluma Gakuen	2	40	1925
Ryukoku Gakuen	5	240	1925
Sanger Gakuen	2	73	1925
Sebastopol Nihongo Gakuen	3	50	1925
Showa Gakuen	1	15	1925
Suisun Nihongo Gakuen	2	56	1925
Vacaville Hogo Gakuen	3	80	1925
Bowless Nihongo Gakuen	2	61	1926
French Camp Nihongo Gakuen	2	87	1926
Kita Sanger Gakuen	2	40	1926
Manmouth Nihongo Gakuen	2	50	1926
Oak Park Doyo Gakuen	3	100	1926
Ofu Kirisutokyo Nihongo Gakuen	4	200	1926
Race Track Hogo Gakuen	1	25	1926
San Ramon Valley Gakuen	1	26	1926
Santa Cruz Hogo Gakuen	1	35	1926
Sunnyside Gakuen	2	21	1926
Clovis Gakuen	1	22	1927
Concord Nihongo Gakuen	2	56	1927
Higashi Florin Nihongo Gakuen	2	35	1927
Meiyu Gakuen	3	63	1927
Obun Nihongo Gakuen	2	65	1927
Showa Juku	1	24	1927
Turlock Hogo Gakuen	1	41	1927
Willow Nihongo Gakuen	1	20	1927
Campbell Nihongo Gakuen	2	39	1928
Gridley Gakuen	1	50	1928
Koyu Gakuen	2	75	1928
Martinez Nihongo Gakuen	1	11	1928
Merced Hogo Gakuen	1	20	1928
San Juan Nihongo Gakuen	2	76	1928
San Martin Chuo Gakuen	1	46	1928

School	Teachers	Students	Established
Stage Gakuen	1	20	1928
Trimbleroad Nihongo Gakuen	2	90	1928
Ashland Gakuen	1	40	1929
Cortez Nihongo Gakuen	2	60	1929
Detalta Gakuen	1	45	1929
Holland Union Gakuen	3	97	1929
Livingstone Nihongo Gakuen	3	30	1929
Loomis Nihongo Gakuen	4	120	1929
Meriken Corner-Nihongo Gakuen	1	51	1929
Cherokee Lane Nihongo Gakuen	1	21	1930
Irvington Nihongo Gakuen	1	22	1930
Linden Hogo Gakuen	1	29	1930
Lochi Gakuen	1	50	1930
Modesto Holiness Kyokai Gakuen	1	15	1930
Riverside Gakuen	1	30	1930
Pescadero Kokugo Gakuen	1	50	1930
Bakersfield Bukkyokai Gakuen	1	52	1931
Bakersfield Nihongo Gakuen	1	48	1931
Higashi Acampo Gakuen	1	70	1931
Berkeley Nihongo Gakko	2	38	1932
Bukkyo-kai Fuzoku Gakuen	2	45	1932
Chico Nihongo Gakuen	2	24	1932
McDonald-to Gakuen	1	31	1932
Nishi Acampo Gakuen	1	40	1932
Rissho Gakuen	3	110	1932
Inoue Ko Gakujuku	2	45	1933
Hollister Gakuen	1	44	1934
Higashi San Jose-Nihongo Gakuen	1	13	1935
Lincoln Nihongo Gakuen	2	60	1935
Bacon Hogo Gakuen	1	21	1936
Baien Gakuen	2	55	1937
Elk Grove Nihongo Gakuen	2	80	–
Parkins Gakuen	2	67	–

Table B–2 Southern California

School	Teachers	Students	Established
Dai-ichi Rafu Gakuen	8	400	1911
Moneta Gakuen	6	250	1912
Oxnard Nihongo Gakuen	1	–	1912

School	Teachers	Students	Established
Rafu Seikokai Nihongo Gakuen	3	107	1914
Talbert Nihongo Gakuen	3	95	1914
Garden Grove Gakuen	2	50	1915
Gardena Hogo Gakuen	3	93	1915
Hollywood Gakuen	5	207	1915
Rafu Dai-ni Gakuen	10	275	1915
Maryknoll Gakuen	5	425	1915
San Gabriel Heigen Nihongo-Gakuen	2	100	1917
Long Beach Nihongo Gakuen	4	113	1918
Rafu Chuo Gakuen	5	300	1918
Rafu Dai-yon Gakuen	3	93	1918
Guadalupe Nihongo Gakuen	3	193	1919
Calexico Gakuen	3	65	1920
Montebello Dai-ni Gakuen	1	15	1920
Santa Maria Nihongo Gakuen	3	45	1921
Baldwin Park Nihongo Gakuen	2	50	1922
Coyote Pass Nihongo Gakuen	2	38	1922
Brawley Bukkyo-kai Gakuen	6	102	1923
Higashi Sanko Seisho Gakuen	5	241	1923
Santa Monica Nihongo Gakuen	2	67	1923
Compton Gakuen	4	75	1924
Pa-shi Nihongo Gakuen	3	97	1924
Anaheim Nihongo Gakuen	1	16	1925
Chula Vista Nihongo Gakuen	2	88	1925
Compton Doyo Gakuen	10	232	1925
Keystone Nihongo Gakuen	4	130	1925
Kita El Monte Nihongo Gakuen	1	53	1925
Lambork Nihongo Gakuen	2	115	1925
Montebello Dai-ichi Gakuen	2	98	1925
Rafu Kirisuto Kyokai-Nihongo Gakuen	5	168	1925
Nishi Hawthorne Gakuen	2	65	1925
Norwalk Nihongo Gkuen	6	240	1925
San Fernando Heigen Nihongo-Gakuen	5	175	1925
Sanko Nihonjin Kumiai Kyokai-Nihongo Gakuen	3	65	1925
Sawtelle Nihongo Gakuen	4	213	1925
Sierra Madre Nihongo Gakuen	1	21	1925
Gardena Bukkyo-kai Gakuen	5	189	1926
Hawthorne Nihongo Gakuen	3	168	1926

School	Teachers	Students	Established
Minami Pasadena Gakuen	2	30	1926
Monrovia Showa Gakuen	1	14	1926
Nihonjin Mii Kokugo Gakuen	5	116	1926
Palos Verdes Nihongo Gakuen	4	80	1926
Pismo Nihongo Gakuen	2	50	1926
Rafu Baptist Gakuen	3	106	1926
Rafu Kokugo Gakko	3	112	1926
Venice Palms Nihongo Gakuen	4	169	1926
Arcadia Nihongo Gakuen	1	26	1927
Arroyo Grande Nihongo Gakuen	2	80	1927
Bandini Gakuen	2	45	1927
Berros Nihongo Gakuen	1	9	1927
Hunger Bukkyo Doyo Gakko	4	115	1927
Minami El Monte Katei Gakuen	1	24	1927
Minato-shi Gakuen	3	85	1927
Nagahama-shi Choro Seisho-Gakuen	2	39	1927
Nishi Torrance Nihongo Gakuen	2	59	1927
Rafu Showa Gakuen	1	40	1927
Santa Barbara Kumiai-Kyokai Nihongo Gakuen	2	50	1927
Coacello no Tomo Kyokai-Gakuen	2	43	1928
Pomona Nihongo Gakuen	1	23	1928
Redondo Futaba Gakuen	3	84	1928
Riverside Gakuen	3	36	1928
Sanko Nihongo Gakuen	2	35	1928
Showa Gakuen	6	137	1928
Wazu Nihongo Gakuen	2	41	1928
Downey Nihongo Gakuen	2	67	1929
Irvine Nihongo Gakuen	2	96	1929
Oxnard Honganji Gakuen	2	84	1929
Pomona Baptist Gakuen	1	29	1929
Santa Barbara Nihongo Gakuen	4	75	1929
Senshin Gakuin	4	185	1929
Vista Nihongo Gakuen	2	64	1929
Wilmington Nihongo Gakuen	3	35	1929
Arlington Nihongo Gakuen	1	30	1930
Coacello Heigen Nihongo-Gakuen	2	22	1930
Fuji Gakuen	2	27	1930
Gun'ei Gijuku	1	30	1930

School	Teachers	Students	Established
Higashi Whittier Nihongo-Gakuen	1	53	1930
Minami El Monte Nihongo-Gakuen	3	42	1930
Otani Gakuen	2	65	1930
Sokei Gakuen	5	345	1930
Ventura Nihongo Gakuen	1	15	1930
Walteria Dai-ni Sokei Gakuen	2	50	1930
Compton Bukkyo Gakuen	2	32	1931
Costa Mesa Nihongo Gakuen	2	45	1931
Hokubei Sogo Gakuen	2	83	1931
Kyoai Nihongo Gakuen	2	25	1931
Midori Nihongo Gakuen	2	50	1931
Rondell Nihongo Gakuen	2	66	1931
Glendale Nihongo Gakuen	2	29	1932
Kita Hollywood Gakuen	2	55	1932
Onodera Jogakko	2	55	1932
Pecho Nihongo Gakuen	1	–	1932
Zoshi Juku	2	60	1932
Mii Kyokai Kokugo Gakuen	1	15	1933
Bassett Nihongo Gakuen	2	80	1934
Rafu Nihongo Chugakko	3	20	1934
Rosemead Nihongo Gakuen	1	28	1935
San Luis Obispo Nihongo-Gakuen	2	41	1935
Meisho Gakuin	3	15	1936
Stanton Nihongo Gakuen	4	102	1936
Yoshin Gakuen	2	69	1936
Baidan Gakuen	4	80	1937
Hinomoto Gakuen	2	50	1938
Nanka Kyoritsu Gakuen	4	90	1938
El Centro Bukkyo-kai Fuzoku-Gakuen	5	130	–
San Diego Bukkyokai Nihongo-Gakuen	4	126	–
Venice Ocean Park-Futaba Gakuen	1	21	–
Winslaw Nihongo Gakuen	7	24	–
Arizona Gakuen	–	–	–
Gallop Gakuen	–	–	–
Hokubei Gakuen	–	–	–
Hollywood Choro Kyokai Gakuen	–	–	–

School	Teachers	Students	Established
Laguna Beach Gakuen	–	–	–
Lomita Gakuen	–	–	–
Los Olas Gakuen	–	–	–
Mesa Gakuen	–	–	–
Mesa Kokugo Gakuen	–	–	–
Niland Gakuen	–	–	–
Rafu Tamagawa Juku	–	–	–
Rancaster Gakuen	–	–	–
San Bernadino Gakuen	–	–	–
San Marino Gakuen	–	–	–
Upland Gakuen	–	–	–

Source: Zaibei Nihonjin-kai Jiseki Hozonbu, *Zaibei Nihonjin-shi* [A History of Japanese in the United States] (San Francisco: Zaibei Nihonjin-kai Jiseki Hozonbu, 1940), 486–493.
*The spelling of the name of some schools is uncertain, due to different ways of reading characters in the original text. The year of establishment varies slightly depending on the source. A dash indicates that no information is available.

Notes

Preface

1. William Morris and Mary Morris, *Morris Dictionary of Word and Phrase Origins* (New York: Harper & Row, 1971), 15–16.
2. David E. Lopez, *Language Maintenance and Shift in the United States Today*, vol. 4 (Los Alamitos, CA: National Center for Bilingual Research, 1982), 53.
3. Yuji Ichioka, Yasuo Sakata, Nobuya Tsuchida, and Eri Yasuhara eds., *Buried Past: An Annotated Bibliography of the Japanese American Research Project Collection* (Berkeley: U of California P, 1974), 3–15.

Chapter 1

1. Robert Paral, *English Only: The Threat of Language Restrictions* (Washington, DC: The NALEO Education Fund, 1989), 3.
2. Joshua A. Fishman, *The Rise and Fall of the Ethnic Revival* (Berlin: Mouton, 1985), 368–370.
3. John Edwards, *Language, Society and Identity* (Oxford: Basil Blackwell, 1985), 96.
4. Edwards 97.
5. Edwards 17.
6. Anne M. Boyran, *Sunday School: The Formation of an American Institution, 1790–1880* (New Haven: Yale UP, 1988), 20.
7. Boyran 6–20.
8. Boyran 23.
9. Boyran 26–30.
10. Boyran 38.
11. James A. Burns, *The Growth and Development of the Catholic School System in the United States* (New York: Benziger Brothers, 1912), 298.
12. David G. Herman, "Neighbors on the Golden Mountain," *DAI* 42/07A (1981): 187.
13. Heinz Kloss, *The American Bilingual Tradition* (Rowley, MA: Newbury House, 1977), 68–69.
14. Burns 297.
15. Burns 70.
16. Herman 265.
17. Alvin I. Schiff, *The Jewish Day School in America* (New York: The Jewish Education Committee of New York, 1966), 203–204.
18. Schiff 247–248.
19. Joshua A. Fishman and Barbara Markman, *The Ethnic Mother-Tongue-School in America: Assumption, Findings, and Directory* (New York: Yeshiva UP, 1979), 199–204.
20. Victor Low, *The Unimpressible Race: A Century of Educational Struggle by the Chinese in San Francisco* (San Francisco: East/West Publishing, 1982), 17.

21. Kim F. Tom, "The Participation of the Chinese in the Community Life of Los Angeles," Master's thesis, USC, 1944, 64.

22. Kim F. Tom, "Function of the Chinese Language School," *Sociology and Social Research* 25:7(1941):561.

23. Asian American Studies Center and Chinese Historical Society of Southern California, *Linking Our Lives: Chinese American Women of Los Angeles* (Los Angeles: UCLA, 1984), 54.

24. Americanization Conference, *Proceedings of the Americanization Conference* (Washington, DC: Bureau of Education, Department of the Interior, 1919). Quoted in Kloss 71.

25. Kloss 71.

26. Japan, The Consulate-General of Japan, San Francisco, *Documental History of Law Cases Affecting Japanese in the United States, 1916–1924* (1925). New York: Arno, 1978), 271–274.

Chapter 2

1. Yamato Ichihashi, *Japanese in the United States* (New York: Arno, 1969), 22.

2. Ichihashi, *Japanese* 24–25.

3. Zaibei Nihonjin-kai Jiseki Hozon-bu, *Zaibei Nihonjin-shi* (San Francisco: Zaibei Nihonjin-kai, 1940), 30.

4. United States Census Office, *Eleventh Census of the United States*, 1890.

5. Ichihashi, *Japanese in the United States*, 1–15.

6. Japan, Gaimusho, *Nihon Gaiko Bunsho, Tai Bei Imin Mondai Keika Gaiyo Fuzokusho* (Tokyo: Gaimusho, 1973), 2.

7. Robert Wilson and Bill Hosokawa, *East to America* (New York: Morrow, 1980), 44.

8. United States Census Office, *Fourteenth Census of the United States*, 1920.

9. Charles M. Wollenberg, *All Deliberate Speed* (Berkeley: U of California P, 1978), 52–53.

10. Matsuzo Nagai, *Nichibei Bunka Kosho-shi*, vol. 5. (Tokyo: Hara-shobo, 1981), 257.

11. Wollenberg 65–66.

12. Japan, Gaimusho 16. *See also* Irving G. Hendrick, *Public Policy Toward the Education of Non-white Minority Group Children in California, 1849–1970* (Riverside: University of California, Riverside, 1975), 82–83.

13. Japan, Gaimusho 21.

14. Reginald Bell, *Public School Education of Second-generation Japanese in California* (1935. New York: Arno Press, 1978), 14–16.

15. Hendrick 85.

16. Wilson and Hosokawa 125.

17. Ichihashi, *Japanese in the United States* 291.

18. Ichihashi, *Japanese in the United States* 321.

19. Soen Yamashita, *Nichi Bei o Tsunagu Mono* (Tokyo: Bunsei-sha, 1938), 64.

20. Kohei Shimano, "Gakuen no Honshitsu o Ronji Wareware no Shoshi o Nobu." In Tenji Nakayama, ed., *Nanka Kyoiku-kai Kaiho Sokango, Dai Nisei no Kyoiku* (Los Angeles: Nanka kyoiku-kai), 1926.

21. For institutional care of Japanese children in Los Angeles, see Makimi Kambayashi, "Issei Women: Life Histories of Six Issei Women Who Participated in Social and Other Activities in Los Angeles, 1984," Master's thesis, UCLA, 1985, 271–289.

22. *Shin Sekai*, April 13, 1908.

23. Hokka Nihongo Gakuen Kyokai, *Beikoku Kashu Nihongo Gakuen Enkaku-shi* (San Francisco: Hokka Nihongo Gakuen Kyokai, 1930), 1. Kazuo Ito claims, however, that it was 1902 when Japanese-language schools were first established in Seattle and San Francisco. *See* Ito Kazuo 592.

24. Japan, Gaimusho Gaiko Shiryo-kan, *Nihongo Gakko Chosa Ikken*, I.1.5.0.13. *Nihongo Gakko Chosa Ikken:* Tokyo: Gaimusho Microfilm.

25. This is based on the following three sources: Japan, Gtaimusho Gaiko Shiryo-kan, I.1.5.0.13. *Nihongo Gakko Chosa Ikken; Zaibei Nihonjin-shi; and Nichi-Bei Bunka Kosho-shi, vol. 5*

26. Tora Uemura, *Hokubei no Nihonjin* (Tokyo: Naigai Shuppan Kyokai, 1912), 129.

27. Takeshi Fukutake ed., *Amerika Mura* (Tokyo: Tokyo Daigaku Shuppankai, 1953), 271–297.

28. Hokka Nihongo Gakuen Kyokai, 8.

29. Edward R. Beauchamp and James M. Vardaman, eds., *Japanese Education since 1945: A Documentary Study* (Armonk, NY: M.E. Sharpe, 1994), 37–38.

30. Herbert Passin, *Society and Education in Japan* (Tokyo: Kodansha International, 1982), 155.

31. Passin 151–152.

32. Hokka Nihongo Gakuen Kyokai 7.

33. Yuji Ichioka, *The Issei: The World of the First Generation Japanese Immigrants, 1885–1924* (New York: Free Press, 1988) 197–200.

34. Tsutae Sato, *Bei-Ka ni okeru Dai-Nisei no Kyoiku* (Vancouver: Jikyo-do, 1932), 1–3.

Chapter 3

1. Edward G. Hartmann, *The Movement to Americanize the Immigrant* (New York: AMS, 1967), 13.

2. Minoru Yoneda, "Zaibei Nihonjin no Ichidai Mondai," *Gaiko Jiho* 26:312 (1917): 20–29.

3. Sato, *Bei Ka* 20.

4. Nagai 263.

5. Taiheiyo Engan Nihonjin Kyogikai *Gijiroku*, 1914–1928. JARP Oversize 81. (N.P.).

6. JARP, *Taiheiyo Engan Nihonjin Kyogikai Gijiroku.*

7. Kiichi Kanzaki, *California and the Japanese* (1921; San Francisco: R and E Research Associates, 1971) 20.

8. State of California, *Resolutions Adopted in an Extra Session of the Forty-third Legislature, 1919* (Sacramento: California State Printing Office, 1921).

9. Herman 612–615.

10. *Rafu Shimpo,* April 24, 1921

11. California State Superintendent of Public Instruction, *Biennial Report* (Sacramento: California State Printing Office, 1922) 27.

12. *Rafu Shimpo,* July 13, July 30, August 26, August 30, September 2, September 10, 1921; March 7, June 26, 1922; January 5, 1923; Zaibei Nihonjin-kai 470.

13. Gladys Waldron, *Antiforeign Movements in California, 1919–1929.* Cited in Herman 616.

14. *Supreme Court Reporter,* October term, 1926, 403–409.

15. Taiheiyo Engan Nihonjin-kai Kyogikai *Gijiroku,* 1914–1928. N.P.

16. Marshall De Motte, "California—White or Yellow?" in *The Annals: Present-day Immigration with Special Reference to the Japanese,* ed. C. Kelsey (Philadelphia: The American Academy of Political and Social Science, 1921), 20.

17. Kelsey 20.

18. Kelsey 20.

19. V. S. McClatchy, "Japanese in the Melting-Pot: Can They Assimilate and Make Good Citizens?" Kelsey 31–32.

20. Kiyoshi. K. Kawakami, *The Real Japanese Question* (New York: Arno, 1921), 143–159.

21. Kawakami 198.

22. Hokka Nihongo Gakuen Kyokai 87.

23. Taiheiyo Engan Nihonjin-kai *Gijiroku* 1914–1928 (N.P.).

24. Kanzaki 21.

25. Hokka Nihongo Gakuen Kyokai 87.

26. Kanzaki 21.

27. Hokka Nihongo Gakuen Kyokai 101.
28. *Rafu Shimpo*, July 2, July 12, 1921.
29. *Rafu Shimpo*, September 20, 1924.
30. *Nichi Bei Shimbun*, May 20, 1927.
31. Kando Ikeda, *Hokubei Hyoron Kirinuki, JARP.*
32. *Rafu Shimpo*, June 27, 1931.
33. *Nihongo Gakko Chosa Ikken.* 1935. Gaiko Shiryo-kan. I.1.5.0.13.
34. *Nichi Bei Shimbun*, November 17, 1931.
35. *Nichi Bei Shimbun*, April 14, 1936.
36. Nanka Shoko Kaigisho, *Minami Kashu Nihonjin 70-nen-shi* (Los Angeles: *Minami Kashu Nihonjin 70-nen-shi Hensan-kai*, 1960), 288.
37. Shia Kyokasho Hensan Suisho Sho (n.d.), (n.p.). *JARP* Box 329.
38. Tomitaro Karasawa, *Kyokasho no Rekishi* (Tokyo: Sobunsha, 1957), 1–18.
39. Shisei Tsuneishi, "Hokubei Haiku no Shorai," *Tachibana* 36, Tsuneishi Papers, *JARP.*
40. Edward K. Strong, *The Second-Generation Japanese Problem* (1934; New York: Arno, 1970), 201–207.
41. John Modell, *The Economics and Politics of Racial Accommodation* (Urbana: U of Illinois P, 1977), 135.
42. Ujiro Oyama, "Beikoku ni okeru Nihongo Gakko Mondai," *Gaiko Jiho* 46:545 (1927):75–83.

Chapter 4

1. Yamashita *Nichi Bei* 50–51.
2. "Japanese," *Harvard Encyclopedia of American Ethnic Groups*, 1980 ed.
3. Wilson and Hosokawa 162.
4. Nagai 257.
5. Jerrold H. Takahashi, "Japanese American Responses to Race Relations: The Formation of Nisei Perspectives," *Amerasia* 9:1 (1982): 31.
6. Yuji Ichioka, "A Study in Dualism: James Yoshinori Sakamoto and the *Japanese American Courier,* 1928–1942," *Amerasia* 13:2 (1986–87): 49–81.
7. *Nichi Bei Shimbun*, September 29, 1931.
8. *Rafu Shimpo*, March 3, 1932.
9. *Rafu Shimpo*, March 3, 1932.
10. *Rafu Shimpo*, April 11, 1933
11. The Japan Times & Mail, *The Truth Behind the Sino-Japanese Crisis: Japan Acts to Keep Eastern Civilization Safe for the World* (Tokyo: The Japan Times & Mail, 1937)
12. Japan Times & Mail 1.
13. "Loyalties: Dual and Divided," *Harvard Encyclopedia of American Ethnic Groups*, 1980 ed.
14. "Education," *Harvard Encyclopedia of American Ethnic Groups*, 1980 ed.
15. Reginald Bell, *Public School Education of Second-generation Japanese in California* (1935; New York: Arno, 1978), 106–107. Bell visited junior and senior high schools with 20 percent or greater Japanese enrollment in Los Angeles, San Diego, Fresno, Stockton, Sacramento, and San Francisco between 1930 and 1931. He then transcribed the academic records of the Japanese pupils, totaling 36,014 marks for 1,823 pupils in 47 high schools and compared them with equivalent records gathered by another researcher on the scholastic achievements of other racial groups in Los Angeles.
16. John Modell, *The Economics and Politics of Racial Accommodation: The Japanese of Los Angeles, 1900–1942* (Urbana: U of Illinois P, 1977), 157.
17. Bell 106–107.
18. Modell 127.
19. Zaibei Nihonjin-kai 502.

20. Passin 62–99.
21. Akiyoshi Hayashida, "Japanese Moral Instruction as a Factor in the Americaniza-
    tion of Citizens of Japanese Ancestry" Master's thesis, U of Hawaii, 1933, 39.
22. "Education," *Harvard Encyclopedia of American Ethnic Groups,* 1980 ed.
23. *Nichi Bei Shimbun,* January 1, 1932.
24. *Nichi Bei Shimbun,* July 17, 1929.
25. *Nichi Bei Shimbun,* January 1, 1936.
26. *Nichi Bei Shimbun,* January 25, 1933
27. *Nichi Bei Shimbun,* March 17, 1932.
28. *Nichi Bei Shimbun,* May 8, 1933.
29. *Nichi Bei Shimbun,* May 30, 1933.
30. *Nichi Bei Shimbun,* October 6, 1928.
31. *Rafu Shimpo,* June 15, 1932.
32. Zaibei Nihonjin-kai Jiseki Hozon-bu, 483–484.
33. Edward K. Strong and Reginald Bell, *Vocational Aptitudes of Second-generation
    Japanese in the United States* (Stanford: Stanford U P, 1933), 114–131.
34. Robert W. O'Brien, *The College Nisei* (1949. New York: Arno, 1978), 11–12.
35. *Rafu Shimpo,* June 15, 1932.
36. *Rafu Shimpo,* September 22, 1932.
37. Sato 12–14.
38. Makoto Aso and Ikuo Amano, *Education and Japan's Modernization* (Tokyo: Japa-
    nese Ministry of Foreign Affairs, 1972), 43–44.
39. Gaiko Shiryo-kan, *Nihongo Gakko Chosa Ikken,* I.1.5.0.13.
40. *Nichi Bei Shimbun,* October 5, 1931
41. *Nichi Bei Shimbun,* August 23, 1937.
42. Kazuo Ito, *Issei: A History of Japanese Immigrants in North America.* Trans.
    Shin'ichiro Nakamura and Jean S. Gerard (Seattle: Executive Committee for
    Publication of Issei, Japanese Community Service, 1973), 596.
43. *Nichi Bei Shimbun,* July 3, 1937.
44. *Nichi Bei Shimbun,* January 9, and January 15, 1932.
45. Tsuneishi Papers. JARP.
46. *Rafu Shimpo,* February 11, 1940.
47. Rafu Shimpo-sha, *Kigen 2600-nen Hoshuku Kinen Taikan,* 28.
48. Rafu Shimpo-sha 28.
49. Rafu Shimpo-sha 52.

Chapter 5

1. Gaimusho, *Nikkei Gaijin Kankei Zakken;* Hiroshima-ken, *Hiroshima-ken Ijushi:
   Shiryohen.* 1992. 703.
2. Harry H. L. Kitano. *Japanese Americans: The Evolution of a Subculture*
   (Englewood Cliffs, NJ: Prentice-Hall, rev. ed., 1976), 159–160.
3. Japan, Gaimusho, *Nihon Gaiko Bunsho.* 1973. 536–538.
4. Yamato Ichihashi, *Japanese in the United States* (New York: Arno, 1969), 322.
5. *Rafu Shimpo.* 25 September 1924; 22 May 1925, 20 September 1925.
6. Nanka Nihongo Gakuen Kyokai, *Kengaku Ryoko Nisshi Kinencho* (Los Angeles:
   Nanka Nihongo Gakuen Kyokai, 1939), 47.
7. Nanka Nihongo Gakuen Kyokai, *Kengaku* 17.
8. Nanka Nihongo Gakuen Kyokai, *Kengaku* 17.
9. Keisen Girls' School, The Nisei Survey Committee, *The Nisei: A Survey of Their
   Educational, Vocational and Social Problems* (Tokyo: Reisen Girls' School, 1939), 19.
10. Keisen 26.
11. Keisen 26–27.
12. Keisen 53–55.
13. Yamashita, *Nichi Bei* 279.
14. Kaigai Kyoiku Kyokai, *An Outline of The Kaigai Kyoiku Kyokai* (The Institute for
    the Education of Overseas Japanese), n.d., 1.

15. Kaigai Kyoiku Kyokai *Outline* 1
16. Kaigai Kyoiku Kyokai, *Zaidan Hojin Kaigai Kyoiko Kyokai Yoram*, 1940. N.P.
17. Kaigai Kyoiku Kyokai *Outline* 7.
18. Strong *Vocational* 114–131.
19. Robert H. Ross, "Social Distance as It Exists between the First and Second Generation Japanese in the City of Los Angeles and Vicinity," Master's thesis, USC, 1939.
20. Ross 61.
21. Ross 61–73.
22. *Nichi Bei Shimbun*, January 1, 1936
23. *Nichi Bei Shimbun*, January 1, 1936.
24. Joseph D. Harrington, *Yankee Samurai: The Secret Role of Nisei in America's Pacific Victory* (Detroit: Pewttingrew Enterprise, 1979), 23.
25. Ichihashi, *Japanese in the United States* 331–332.
26. Kitano 27.
27. *Nichi Bei Shimbun*, December 10, 1936.
28. Soen Yamashita, *Nikkei Shimin no Nihon Ryugaku Jijo* (Tokyo: Bunseisha, 1935), 176–209.
29. Miya Kikuchi, "A Letter to Robert A. Wilson, Director JARP, UCLA, 13 January 1968," *JARP.*
30. *Nichi Bei Shimbun*, July 5, 1937.
31. Yamashita, *Nikkei Shimin no Nihon Ryugaku Jijo* 190–191.

Chapter 6

1. Ichihashi points out that there is disagreement as to the number in the first group of Japanese immigrants, varying from 48 to 153, according to different accounts. See Ichihashi, *The Japanese in the United States* 22–23 for more details.
2. Ichihashi, *The Japanese in the United States* 24–25.
3. Ichihashi, *The Japanese in the United States* 31–34.
4. Yoshihide Matsubayashi, "The Japanese Language Schools in Hawaii and California from 1892 to 1941." *DAI* 46 (1985): 1540A, U of San Francisco.
5. Hawai Nihonjin Rengo Kyokai, *Hawai Nihonjin Imin-shi* (Honolulu: United Japanese Society of Hawaii, 1977), 232.
6. Hawai Nihonjin Rengo Kyokai 232.
7. Hawai Nihonjin Rengo Kyokai 234.
8. Matsubayashi 83–113.
9. Matsubayashi 139–143.
10. Hawai Nihonjin Rengo Kyokai 240–242; John N. Hawkins, "Politics, Education, and Language Policy: The Case of Japanese Language Schools in Hawaii." *Amerasia*, 5.1(1978):39–56; Matsubayashi 139–184.
11. Hawai Nihonjin Rengo Kyokai 243–246.
12. Hawkins 53–54.
13. Nobuya Tsuchida, "The Japanese in Brazil, 1908–1941." *DAI* 39/09A (1978): 5676, UCLA, 132–133.
14. Tomoo Handa, *Imin no Seikatsu no Rekishi: Burajiru Nikkeijin no Ayunda Michi* (São Paulo: Centro de Estudos Nipo Brasileiros, 1970), 306–310.
15. Tsuchida 227–243.
16. Tsuchida 235.
17. Handa 611.
18. *Jiho*, October 21, 1938. *Burajiru Nihon Imin Shiryo-kan Shozo Bunsho Shiryo.*
19. *Seiho*, November 9, 1938. *Burajiru Nihon Imin Shiryo-kan Shozo Bunsho Shiryo.*
20. *Nippaku*, December 24, 1938. *Burajiru Nihon Imin Shiryo-kan Shozo Bunsho Shiryo.*
21. Handa 611–614. For discussion related to the nationalistic movement among the Japanese immigrants in Brazil in the 1940s, see Takashi Maeyama, *Imin no Nihon Kaiki Undo* (Tokyo: Nihon Hoso Shuppan-kyokai, 1982).

22. Nihongo Fukyu Senta, *Nihongo Gakko Shozai Bunpu Ichiran*, (São Paulo: Nihongo Fukyu Senta, 1987), 1.
23. Tsuchida 1.
24. Nippaku Bunka Renmei, ed., *Densho eno Michi: Burajiru Shakai ga Yokyu suru Nihongo Kyoiku to Sono Tenbo* (São Paulo: Nippaku Bunka Renmei, 1982), 30–31.

Chapter 7

1.   Thomas James, *Exile Within: The Schooling of Japanese Americans, 1942–1945* (Cambridge, MA: Harvard UP, 1987), 82–84.
2.   James 149.
3.   James 153.
4.   The California Association of Japanese Language Schools, Inc. *By-Laws*. n.p., n.d.
5.   *Shin Nichi-Bei* [New Japanese American News], May 4, 1965. Japanese-language schools had to wait another year until the bill was actually in effect. Furthermore, it was required that students take an examination to earn credits.
6.   Lopez 52–53.
7.   Fishman and Markman 303.
8.   Joshua Fishman et al., *Language Loyalty in the United States: The Maintenance and Perpetuation of Non-English Mother Tongues by American Ethnic and Religious Groups* (The Hague: Mouton, 1966), 118.
9.   The California Association of Japanese Language Schools.
10. Fishman and Markman 209.
11. Fishman and Markman 209.
12. Nihongo Gakuen Kyodo System, *1987 Kyodo System Annual Report* (Los Angeles: Nihongo Gakuen Kyodo System, 1988), 1–3.
13. The survey was conducted in conjunction with *Shumi no Matsuri*, an annual event for exhibitions at the school.
14. Edwards 100.
15. Japan, Mombusho, *Waga Kuni no Bunkyo Seisaku* (Tokyo: Okura-sho Insatsukyoku, 1993), 479–486.
16. The *Rafu Shimpo*, December 16, 1980.
17. Roger Goodman, "The Problem of the Problem of Japan's Returnee School Children," *Proceedings of the British Association for Japanese Studies*, 1986, 11.

Epilogue

1.   Fishman, *Language Loyalty* 21–22.
2.   Kitano 3.
3.   Russell N. Campbell and Kathryn J. Lindholm, *Conservation of Language Resources* (Los Angeles: Center for Language Education and Research, UCLA, 1987), 6.
4.   Barbara F. Freed, "The Foreign-Language Requirement." *Teaching Languages in College: Curriculum and Content*, ed. Wilga M. Rivers (Lincolnwood, IL: National Textbook Company, 1992), 42.

Bibliography

In English

Americanization Conference. *Proceedings of the American Conference, Washington, DC: Bureau of Education, Department of the Interior, 1919.*

Asian American Studies Center and Chinese Historical Society of Southern California. *Linking Our Lives: Chinese American Women of Los Angeles.* Los Angeles: UCLA, 1984.

Aso, Makoto and Ikuo Amano. *Education and Japan's Modernization.* Tokyo: Japanese Ministry of Foreign Affairs, 1972.

Beauchamp, Edward R. and James M. Vardaman, eds. *Japanese Education since 1945: A Documentary Study.* Armonk, NY: M.E. Sharpe, 1994.

Bell, Reginald. *Public School Education of Second-Generation Japanese in California.* 1935. New York: Arno, 1978.

Bonacich, Edna and John Modell. *The Economic Basis of Ethnic Solidarity: Small Business in the Japanese American Community.* Berkeley: U of California P, 1980.

Boyran, Anne M. *Sunday School: The Formation of an American Institution, 1790–1880.* New Haven: Yale UP, 1988.

Burns, James A. *The Growth and Development of the Catholic School System in the United States: Its Principles, Origin, and Establishment.* New York: Benziger Brothers, 1912.

California. *Report of Senate Fact-Finding Committee on Japanese Settlement.* Sacramento: California State Printing Office, 1945.

——. *State Superintendent of Public Instruction. Biennial Report.* Sacramento: California State Printing Office, 1922.

——. Statute of California. *Resolutions Adopted at Extra Session of the Forty-third Legislature, 1921.* Sacramento: California State Printing Office, 1921.

Campbell, Russell and Kathryn J. Lindholm. *Conservation of Language Resources.* Educational Report Series 6. Los Angeles: Center for Language Education and Research, UCLA, 1978.

Casey, Christine. "Ethnic Identity and Self-Esteem in Second and Third Generation Polish and Italian Sixth Grade Children." *DAI* 46/11A (1985): 3273.

Cortínez, Verónica. "The Excitement of Literature: A Lifelong Pursuit." *Teaching Languages in College: Curriculum and Content.* Ed. Wilga M. Rivers. Lincolnwood, IL: National Textbook Company, 1992.

Cruttenden, Kim Margaret. "A Descriptive Study of Three Ethnic Chinese Schools." MA thesis, UCLA, 1986.

"Education." *Harvard Encyclopedia of American Ethnic Groups,* 1980 ed.

Edwards, John. *Language, Society and Identity.* Oxford: Basil Blackwell, 1985.

Fan, Chen Y. "The Chinese Language School of San Francisco in Relation to Family Integration and Cultural Identity." *DAI* 37/12 (1976): 7414A. Duke University.

162 Bibliography

Fishman, Joshua A. "Bilingual Education in the United States under Ethnic Community Auspices." *Georgetown University Round Table on Language and Linguistics: Current Issues in Bilingual Education.* Ed. James E. Alatis. Washington, DC: Georgetown UP, 1980.

———. *Non-English Language Resources of the United States.* Final Report. New York: Yeshiva UP, 1980.

———. *The Rise and Fall of the Ethnic Revival: Perspectives on Language and Ethnicity.* Berlin: Mouton, 1985.

Fishman, Joshua A., et al. *Language Loyalty in the United States: The Maintenance and Perpetuation of Non-English Mother Tongues by American Ethnic and Religious Groups.* The Hague: Mouton, 1966.

Fishman, Joshua A., and Barbara Markman. *The Ethnic Mother-Tongue-School in America: Assumption, Findings, and Directory.* New York: Yeshiva UP, 1979.

Freed, Barbara F. "The Foreign-Language Requirement." *Teaching Languages in College: Curriculum and Content.* Ed. Wilga M. Rivers. Lincolnwood, IL: National Textbook Company, 1992.

Goodman, Roger. "The Problem of the Problem of Japan's Returnee School Children." *Proceedings of the British Association of Japanese Studies,* 1986.

Grosjean, François. *Life with Two Languages: An Introduction to Bilingualism.* Cambridge, MA: Harvard UP, 1982.

Harrington, Joseph D. *Yankee Samurai: The Secret Role of Nisei in America's Pacific Victory.* Detroit, MI: Pettingrew Enterprises, 1979.

Hartmann, E. G. *The Movement to Americanize the Immigrant. 1948.* New York: AMS, 1967.

Hawkins, John N. "Politics, Education, and Language Policy: The Case of Japanese Language Schools in Hawaii." *Amerasia* 5:1, 1978: 39–56.

Hayashida, Akiyoshi. "Japanese Moral Instruction as a Factor in the Americanization of Citizens of Japanese Ancestry." MA thesis, U of Hawaii, 1933.

Hendrick, Irving G. *Public Policy Toward the Education of Non-white Minority Group Children in California, 1849–1970.* Riverside: U of California P, 1975.

Herman, David G. "Neighbors on the Golden Mountain: The Americanization of Immigrants in California Public Instruction as an Agency of Ethnic Assimilation, 1850 to 1933." *DAI* 42/07A (1981):3037A U of California P, Berkeley.

Hirota, P. T. *Orations and Essays by the Japanese Second Generation of America.* Los Angeles: The Los Angeles Japanese Daily News, 1932.

Ichihashi, Yamato. *Japanese Immigration: Its Status in California.* San Francisco: The Marshall Press, 1915.

———. *The Japanese in the United States: A Critical Study of the Problems of the Japanese Immigrants and Their Children. 1932.* New York: Arno, 1969.

Ichioka, Yuji, Yasuo Sakata, Nobuya Tsuchida, and Eri Yasuhara, eds. *Buried Past: An Annotated Bibliography of the Japanese American Research Project Collection.* Berkeley: U of California P, 1974.

Ichioka, Yuji. "Study in Dualism: James Yoshinori Sakamoto and the *Japanese American Courier,* 1928–1942." *Amerasia* 9:1, 1982.

———. *The Issei: The World of the First Generation Japanese Immigrants, 1885–1924.* New York: Free, 1988.

Isaacs, Harold R. *Idols of the Tribe: Group Identity and Political Change.* New York: Harper Colophon Books, 1975.

Ito, Kazuo. *Issei: A History of Japanese Immigrants in North America.* Trans. Shin'ichiro Nakamura and Jean S. Gerard. Seattle: Executive Committee for Publication of Issei, Japanese Community Service, 1973.

James, Thomas. "The Education of Japanese Americans at Tule Lake, 1942–1946." *Pacific Historical Review,* 56 (1987): 25–58.

———. *Exile Within: The Schooling of Japanese Americans, 1942–1946.* Cambridge, MA: Harvard UP, 1987.

Japan. The Consulate-General of Japan, San Francisco. *Documental History of Law Cases Affecting Japanese in the United States, 1916–1924.* 1925. New York: Arno, 1978.

The Japan Times & Mail. *The Truth Behind the Sino-Japanese Crisis: Japan Acts to Keep Eastern Civilization Safe for the World.* Tokyo: The Japan Times & Mail, 1937.

"Japanese." *Harvard Encyclopedia of American Ethnic Groups,* 1980 ed.

Jung, Raymond K. "The Chinese Language School in the U.S." *School & Society* 100 (1972): 309–311.

Kambayashi, Makimi. "Issei Women: Life Histories of Six Issei Women Who Participated in Social and Other Activities in Los Angeles, 1989." MA thesis, UCLA, 1985.

Kanzaki, Kiichi. *California and the Japanese.* 1921. San Francisco: R and E Research Associates, 1971.

Kawakami, Kiyoshi. K. *The Real Japanese Question.* New York: Arno, 1921.

Keisen Girls' School, The Nisei Survey Committee. *The Nisei: A Survey of Their Educational Vocational and Social Problems.* Tokyo: Keisen Girls' School, 1939.

Kelsey, Carl. *The Annals: Present-Day Immigration with Special Reference to the Japanese.* Philadelphia: The American Academy of Political and Social Science, 1921.

Kitano, Harry H. L. *Japanese American: The Evolution of a Subculture.* rev. ed. Englewood Cliffs, NJ: Prentice-Hall, 1976.

Kloss, Heinz. *The American Bilingual Tradition.* Rowley, MA: Newbury House, 1977.

Kuznicki, Ellen. M. "An Ethnic School in American Education: A Study of the Origin, Development, and Sisters in the Polish American Catholic Schools of Western New York." *DAI* 13/12A (1973): 6845.

Levine, Gene N., and Colbert Rhodes. *The Japanese American Community: A Three-Generation Study.* New York: Praeger, 1981.

Lopez, David E. *Language Maintenance and Language Shift in the United States Today: The Basic Patterns and Their Social Implications, Vol. 4.* Los Alamitos, CA: National Center for Bilingual Research, 1982.

Low, Victor. *The Unimpressible Race: A Century of Educational Struggle by the Chinese in San Francisco.* San Francisco: East/West Publishing, 1982.

"Loyalties: Dual and Divided." *Harvard Encyclopedia of American Ethnic Groups,* 1980 ed.

Matsumoto, Valerie J. *Farming the Home Place: A Japanese American Community in California, 1919–1982.* Ithaca: Cornell UP, 1993.

Matsubayashi, Yoshihide. "The Japanese Language Schools in Hawaii and California from 1892 to 1941." *DAI* 46 (1985): 1540A. U of San Francisco.

Mills, Harry A. *The Japanese Problems in the United States.* New York: Macmillan, 1915.

Minoura, Yasuko. "Life in-between: The Acquisition of Cultural Identity among Japanese Children Living in the United States." *DAI* 44/11A (1979): 5922. UCLA.

Modell, John. *The Economics and Politics of Racial Accommodation: The Japanese of Los Angeles, 1900–1942.* Urbana: U of Illinois P, 1977.

Montero, Darrell. *Japanese Americans: Changing Patters of Ethnic Affiliation over Three Generations.* Boulder, CO: Westview, 1980.

Morris, William and Mary Morris. *Morris Dictionary of Word and Phrase Origins.* New York: Harper & Row, 1971.

Nihongo Gakuen Kyodo System. *1987 Kyodo System Annual Report.* Los Angeles: Nihongo Gakuen Kyodo System, 1988.

O'Brien, Robert W. *The College Nisei.* 1949. New York: Arno, 1978.

Paral, Robert. *English Only: The Threat of Language Restrictions.* Washington, DC: The NALEO Education Fund, 1989.

Passin, Herbert. *Society and Education in Japan.* 1965. Tokyo: Kodansha International, 1982.

Rivers, Wilga M., ed. *Teaching Languages in College: Curriculum and Content.* Lincolnwood, IL: National Textbook Company, 1992.

Ross, Robert H. "Social Distance as It Exists between the First and Second Generation Japanese in the City of Los Angeles and Vicinity." MA thesis. U of Southern California, 1939.

Schiff, Alvin I. *The Jewish Day School in America*. New York: Jewish Education Committee of New York P, 1966.

Shibata, Grace S. "Ethnic Japanese Language Schools in the Los Angeles Area: A Descriptive Study." MA thesis. UCLA, 1988.

Simon, Paul. *The Tongue-tied American*. New York: The Crossroad Publishing, 1980.

Strong, Edward K. and Reginald Bell. *Vocational Aptitudes of Second-Generation Japanese in the United States*. Stanford University Press, 1933.

————. *The Second-Generation Japanese Problem*. 1934. New York: Arno, 1970.

Takahashi, Jerrold H. "Japanese American Responses to Race Relations: The Formation of Nisei Perspectives." *Amerasia* 9:1, 1982.

Thomas, Dorothy S. *The Salvage*. Berkeley: U of California P, 1952.

Tom, Kim F. "Function of the Chinese Language School." *Sociology and Social Research* 25:7 (1941): 557–571.

————. "The Participation of the Chinese in the Community Life of Los Angeles." MA thesis. U of Southern California, 1944.

Tsuboi, Sakae. "The Japanese Language School Teacher." *Sociology and Social Research* 11 (1926): 160–165.

Tsuchida, Nobuya. "The Japanese in Brazil, 1908–1941." *DAI* 39/09A (1978): 5676.

United States Census Office. *Eleventh Census of the United States*, 1890.

————. *Fourteenth Census of the United States*, 1920.

United States House of Representatives. *Sixty-sixth Congress, Japanese Immigration Hearings before the Committee on Immigration and Naturalization, Part 2*. Washington: Government Printing Office, 1921.

United States Supreme Court. *Supreme Court Reporter*, October term, 1926.

Wakatsuki, Yasuo. "Japanese Emigration to the United States, 1866–1924." *Perspectives in American History*. Ed. F. Donald. Cambridge: The Charles Warren Center for Studies in American History, Harvard UP, 1979.

Weinreich, Uriel. *Languages in Contact: Findings and Problems*. Berlin: Mouton, 1963.

Wilson, Robert A., and Bill Hosokawa. *East to America*. New York: Morrow, 1980.

Wilson, Woodrow, Franklin K. Lane, and Theodore Roosevelt. *Americanism*. Washington, DC: Americanization Department, 1915.

Wollenberg, Charles M. *All Deliberate Speed*. Berkeley: U of California P, 1978.

In Japanese

Fujioka, Shimei. *Minzoku Hatten no Senkusha* [Pioneers of National Development]. Tokyo: Dobun-sha, 1927.

————. *Ayumi no Ato* [Traces of a Journey]. Los Angeles: Ayumi no Ato Kanko Koenkai, 1957.

Handa, Tomoo. *Imin no Seikatsu no Rekishi: Burajiru Nikkeijin no Ayunda Michi* [A History of the Life of Japanese Immigrants in Brazil]. São Paulo: Centro de Estudos Nipo Brasileiros, 1970.

Hawai Nihonjin Rengo Kyokai. *Hawai Nihonjin Imin-shi* [A History of Japanese Immigrants in Hawaii]. Honolulu: United Japanese Society of Hawaii, 1964.

Hiroshima-ken, ed. *Hiroshima-ken Iju-shi, Shiryo-hen* [A History of Emigrants from Hiroshima, Materials]. Tokyo: Dai-ichi Hoki, 1991.

Imai, Teruko and Yoko Murakawa. "Beikoku Taiheiyogan Shoshu ni okeru Nihongo Kyoiku oyobi sono Bunka Hen'yo ni kansuru Ichi Oboegaki" [A Pattern of Acculturation of Japanese Education in the United States]. *Tsudajuku Daigaku Kiyo* [Journal of Tsuda College] 17 (1985): 91–102.

Japan. Gaimusho. *Nihon Gaiko Bunsho, Tai Bei Imin Mondai Keika Gaiyo Fuzoku-sho* [Diplomatic Records: An Overview of the Problems with the United States]. Tokyo: Gaimusho, 1973.

————. Ryoji Iju-bu. *Waga Kokumin no Kaigai Hatten, Shiryo-hen* [Overseas Development of Japanese Materials]. Tokyo: Gaimusho, 1971.

Japan. Gaimusho Gaiko Shiryo-kan [Ministry of Foreign Affairs, Diplomatic Record Office]. *I.1.5.0.13. Nihongo Gakko Chosa Ikken* [A Survey of Japanese-Language Schools]. Tokyo: Gaimusho Microfilm.

———. *K.1.1.0.9. Nikkei Gaijin Kankei Zakken* [Miscellaneous Documents relating to the Alien Japanese]. Tokyo: Gaimusho Microfilm.

———. Mombusho. *Waga Kuni no Bunkyo Seisaku* [Educational Policy in Japan]. Tokyo: Okura-sho Insatsu-kyoku, 1993.

Kaigai Kyoiku Kyokai. *An Outline of the Kaigai Kyoiku Kyokai* [The Institute for the Education of Overseas Japanese]. N.d., n.p.

Karasawa, Tomitaro. *Kyokasho no Rekishi* [History of Textbooks]. Tokyo: Sobun-sha, 1956.

Kato, Shin'ichi. *Amerika Imin Hyakunen-shi* [The One-Hundred Year History of the Japanese in the United States]. Tokyo: Jiji Tsushin-sha, 1962.

Kumei, Teruko. *Gaikokujin o meguru Shakai-shi: Kindai Amerika to Nihonjin Imin* [A Social History of Foreigners: Modern America and Japanese Immigrants]. Tokyo: Yusan-kaku, 1995.

Kobayashi, Tetsuya. *Ibunka ni Sodatsu Kodomo-tachi* [Children Growing Up in Other Cultures]. Tokyo: Yubikaku, 1983.

Kojima, Masaru. *Dai-Niji Sekai Taisen Mae no Zaigai Shitei Kyoiku-ron no Keifu, Ryukoku Sosho I* [A History of Japanese Children Abroad Prior to World War II, Ryukoku Sosho Vol. 1]. Kyoto: Ryukoku Gakkai, 1993.

Kyodo System Ko-Chu Gakubu. *Ko-Chu Gakubu 30-shunen Kinen-shi* [Ko-chu Gakubu 30th Anniversary Booklet] Los Angeles: Kyodo System Ko-Chu Gakubu, 1986.

Maeyama, Takashi. *Imin no Nihon Kaiki Undo* [The Return-to-Japan Movement of Japanese Immigrants in Brazil]. Tokyo: Nihon Hoso Shuppan Kyokai, 1982.

Nagai, Matsuzo, ed. *Nichi Bei Bunka Kosho-shi* [A History of Japan–U.S. Negotiations]. Vol. 5: Iju [Immigration]. Tokyo: Hara-shobo, 1981.

Nakagawa, Musho. *Zaibei Toshiroku* [The Japanese Pioneers in the United States]. Los Angeles: Hakubun-do Shoten, 1932.

Nanka Nikkeijin Shoko Kaigi-sho. *Minami Kashu Nihonjin 70-nen-shi* [The Seventy-Year-History of the Japanese in Southern California]. Los Angeles: Minami Kashu Nihonjin 70-nen-shi Hensan-kai, 1960.

Nihongo Fukyu Senta. *Nihongo Gakko Shozai Bunpu Ichiran* [A List of Japanese Language Schools]. São Paulo: Nihongo Fukyu Senta, 1987.

Niisato, Kan'ichi. *Zai Bei no Nihon Minzoku 500-nen no Taikei* [A 500-Year Plan for the Japanese in America]. Tokyo: Shimpo-sha, 1940.

Nippaku Bunka Renmei, ed., *Densho eno Michi: Burajiru Shakai ga Yokyu suru Nihongo Kyoiku to sono Tenbo* [A Road to Transmitting Our Culture: What Brazilian Society Demands of Japanese-Language Education, and Prospects for the Future]. São Paulo: Nippaku Bunka Renmei, 1982.

Rafu Shimpo-sha, ed. *Kigen 2600-nen Hoshuku Kinen Taikan* [The Commemorating Volume for the 2600th Anniversary of the Founding of Japan]. Los Angeles: Rafu Shimpo-sha, 1940.

Sakata, Yasuo, ed. *Fading Footsteps of the Issei: An Annotated Check List of the Manuscript Holdings of the Japanese American Research Project Collection.* Los Angeles: Asian American Studies Center and Center for Japanese Studies, UCLA; and Japanese American National Museum, 1992.

Sato, Tsutae. *Bei Ka ni okeru Dai-Nisei no Kyoiku* [Education for the Second Generation in the United States and Canada]. Vancouver: Jikyo-do, 1932.

Tanaka, Keijiro. *Kyoiku ni okeru Bunkateki Doka* [Cultural Assimilation in Education]. Tokyo: Honpo-sha, 1985.

Wakatsuki, Yasuo. *Hainichi no Rekishi* [A History of the Anti-Japanese Movement]. Tokyo: Chuko Shinsho, 1972.

Washizu, Shakuma. *Zaibei Nihonjin Shikan* [A Historical View of the Japanese in the United States]. Los Angeles: Rafu Shimpo-sha, 1930.

Yoneyama, Hiroshi. "Dai-niji Sekai Taisen Mae no Nikkei Nisei to 'Americanism.' [The Second Generation Japanese Americans Prior to World War II and 'Americanism'." *Amerika Kenkyu* 20 (1986): 99–113.

Zaibei Nihonjin-kai Jiseki Hozon-bu. *Zaibei Nihonjin-shi* [A History of Japanese in the United States]. San Francisco: Zaibei Nihonjin-kai, 1940.

Newspapers (Microfilm)

Jiho. Burajiru Nihon Imin Shiryo-kan Shozo Bunsho Shiryo [Documents of the Japanese-Brazilian Historical Museum]. 1938. Tokyo: Nihon Maikuro Shashin Kabushikigaisha, 1987.

Nichi Bei Shimbun [Japanese American News]. San Francisco. 1927–1937.

Nippaku. Burajiru Nihon Imin Shiryo-kan Shozo Bunsho Shiryo [Documents of the Japanese-Brazilian Historical Museum]. 1938. Tokyo: Nihon Maikuro Shashin Kabushikigaisha, 1987.

Rafu Shimpo [Los Angeles Japanese Daily News]. Los Angeles. Microfilm, UCLA. 1921–1933, 1940, 1980.

Seiho. Burajiru Nihon Imin Shiryo-kan Shozo Bunsho Shiryo [Documents of the Japanese-Brazilian Historical Museum]. 1938. Tokyo: Nihon Maikuro Shashin Kabushikigaisha, 1987.

Shin Nichi-Bei [New Japanese American News]. May 4, 1965.

Shinsekai [New World Daily]. San Francisco. Microfilm, UCLA. 1908.

Tokyo Asahi Shimbun. 1932, 1933.

Japanese American Research Project Collections

Aoyagi, Ikutaro, ed. *Zaigai Hojin Dai-Nisei Mondai, Dai-isshu* [Problems of the Second Generation Overseas Japanese, Part 1]. Tokyo: Imin Mondai Kenkyu-kai, 1940.

Beikoku Seihoku-bu Renraku Nihonjin-kai. *Kaimu Hokoku* [Minutes], March 1–August 31, 1921.

Endo, Koshiro. *Kengaku Ryoko Nisshi Kinencho* [Souvenir Album of an Educational Excursion]. Los Angeles: Nanka Nihongo Gakuen Kyokai, 1939.

Hawai Hochi-sha. *Nihongo Gakko Shoso Jusshu-nen Kinen-shi* [Tenth Anniversary of the Victory of the Japanese Language School Litigation], 1937.

Hawai Kyoiku-kai Hensan-bu. *Hawai Nihongo Kyoiku-shi* [History of Japanese Language Education in Hawaii], 1937.

Hokka Nihongo Gakuen Kyokai. *Beikoku Kashu Nihongo Gakuen Enkaku-shi* [Outline History of Japanese Language Schools in California], 1930.

Hoshimiya Family Papers. N.d., n.p.

Ikeda, Kando. *Hokubei Hyoron Kirinuki* [North American Review clippings]. n.d.

Matsuoka, Tadaichi. "Zaibei Nihonjin Dai-Nisei wa Doko e Yuku [Where is the Second Generation Japanese in America Going?]. *Gaiko Jiho* [Revue Diplomatique] 61:650 (1932): 276–286. Microfilm.

Naito, Keizo, ed. *Zaidan Hojin Kaigai Kyoiku Kyokai Yoran* [Association for the Education of Overseas Japanese: An Outline]. Kawasaki: Zaidan Hojin Kaigai Kyoiku-kyokai, 1940.

Nakayama, Tenji, ed. *Dai-Nisei no Kyoiku* [The Education of the Second Generation]. Los Angeles: Nanka Kyoiku-kai, 1926.

Nanka Nihongo Gakuen Kyokai. *Dai-Nisei Nihongo Sakubun-shu* [Collection of Nisei Compositions in Japanese]. Los Angeles: Nanka Nihongo Gakuen Kyokai , 1939.

Nihon Beifu Kyokai. *Dai-Nisei to Kokuseki Mondai: Dai-Nisei Sosho, Dai-3-shu* [The Nisei and the Problem of Nationality, Nisei Book Series No. 3]. Tokyo: Runbini, 1938.

———. *Nihon Ryugaku no Atarashiki Hoho: Dai-Nisei Sosho, Dai 9-shu* [A New Approach to Study in Japan, Nisei Book Series, No. 9]. Tokyo: Runbini, 1938.

Oyama, Ujiro. "Beikoku ni okeru Nihongo Gakko Mondai" [Japanese Language School Problems in the United States]. *Gaiko Jiho* [Revue Diplomatique]. 46:545 (1927): 75–83.

Rafu Uwa-machi Dai-Ni Gakuen. *Rafu Uwa-machi Dai-ni Gakuen-shi* [History of the Los Angeles Nippon Institute], 1965.

Taiheiyo Engan Nihonjin Kyogikai. *Gijiroku* [Minutes], 1914–1928.

Terami Papers, N.d., n.p.

Tsunemitsu, Kozen. *Nihon Ryugaku no Jissai* [Facts about Studying in Japan]. Tokyo: Runbini Shuppan, 1936.

Tsuneishi, Shisei. "Hokubei Haiku no Shorai," [Future of Haiku in North America] *Tachibana* 36 (2) (1969).

Uemura, Tora. *Hokubei no Nihonjin* [The Japanese in the United States]. Tokyo: Naigai Shuppan Kyokai, 1912. Microfilm.

Yamada, Tatsumi. *Kaigai Dai-Nisei Mondai* [Problems of the Overseas Nisei]. Tokyo: Kibundo, 1936. Microfilm.

Yamashita, Soen. *Nikkei Shimin no Nihon Ryugaku Jijo* [The State of Japanese Americans Studying in Japan]. Tokyo: Bunsei-sha, 1935. Microfilm.

————. *Nichi-Bei o Tsunagu Mono* [Those Who Link Japan and the United States]. Tokyo: Bunsei-sha, 1938. Microfilm.

Yoneda, Minoru. "Zaibei Nihonjin no Ichidai Mondai." [Critical Issues among the Japanese in America] *Gaiko Jiho* [Revue Diplomatique], 26:312 (1917): 20–29.

Japanese Textbooks

For the complete list of holdings of the Japanese American Research Project, see Yuji Ichioka, Yasuo Sakata, Nobuya Tsuchida, Eri Yasuhara, eds., *A Buried Past: An Annotated Bibliography of the Japanese American Research Project Collection* (Berkeley: U of California P, 1974) and Yasuo Sakata, ed., *Finding Footsteps of the Issei: An Annotated Check List of the Manuscript Holdings of the Japanese American Research Project Collection* (Los Angeles: Asian American Studies Center and Center for Japanese Studies, UCLA; and Japanese American National Museum, 1992).

Kawamura, Yusen, ed. *Amerika Nihongo Tokuhon* [The American Japanese-Language Reader]. San Francisco: Beikoku Nikkei Jido Kyoiku Kenkyu-kai, 1935.

Mihara, Tokinobu. and Ester Y. Tani. *Japanese Reader: Rendered into Roman Characters and Translated into English from the Textbooks of the Elementary School in Japan.* San Francisco: Sutter St. Printing, 1940.

Nakayama, Tenji. *Haha no Kotoba* [The Mother's Tongue]. Los Angeles: Nakayama Tenju Shuppan-sha, 1924.

Nihongo Gakuen Hensan Iin-kai. *Nihongo Tokuhon* [The Japanese-Language Reader] Vols. 1,2,4,11,13. San Francisco: Aoki Taisei-do, 1930–1939.

Index